HOW TO CHANGE EVERYTHING

Life Only Starts When You Make Things Happen

Velma Gibbs

Table of Contents

Chapter 1:

The People You Need in Your Life

We all have friends, the people that are there for us and would be there no matter what. These people don't necessarily need to be different, and these traits might all be in one person. Friends are valuable. You only really ever come across ones that are real. In modern-day society, it's so hard to find friends that want to be your friends rather than just to use you.

Sometimes the few the better, but you need some friends that would guide you along your path. We all need them, and you quite possibly have these traits too. Your friends need you, and you may not even know it.

1. The Mentor

No matter which area or field they are trying to excel in, the common denominator is that they have clarity about life and know exactly what their goals are. These people can impact you tremendously, helps you get into the winners' mindset, infuse self-belief and confidence in you then you, too, can succeed and accomplish your goals. They act as a stepping stone for you to get through your problems. They are happy for your success and would guide you through the troubles and problems while trying to get there.

2. Authentic People

You never feel like you have to make pretense around these people. Life can be challenging enough, so having friends that aren't judging you and are being themselves is very important for your well-being. This type of friend allows you to be vulnerable, express your emotion in healthy ways, and helps bring a smile back to your face when you're down.

They help you also show your true self and how you feel. Rather than showing only a particular side of their personality, they open their whole self to you, allowing you to do the same and feel comfortable around them.

3. Optimists

These people are the kind you need, the ones that will encourage you through tough times. They will be there encouraging you, always seeing the best in the situation. Having the ability to see the best in people and will always have an open mind to situations. Everyone needs optimism in their lives, and these people bring that.

"Optimism is essential to achievement, and it is also the foundation of courage and true progress." -Nicholas M. Butler.

4. Brutally Honest People

To have a balanced view of yourself and be aware of your blind spots is important for you. Be around people who would provide authentic feedback and not sugarcoat while giving an honest opinion about you. They will help you be a better version of yourself, rectifying your mistakes, work on your weak spots, and help you grow. These are the people you can hang around to get better, and you will critique yourself but in a good way, helping you find the best version of yourself. Of course, the ones that are just rude should be avoided, and they should still be nice to you but not too nice to the point where they compliment you even when they shouldn't.

Chapter 2:

Visualise Your Success In Life

When you have a clear idea of what you want in life, it becomes easier to achieve somehow. When you visualize yourself doing something, you automatically tend to get the results better. You can imagine your success in your mind before you even reach it so that it gives you a sense of comfort. You get the confidence that you can do whatever you desire. You complete your task more quickly because you have already done it once in your mind before even starting it. It relaxes us so we can interpret the outcome. You dream about your goals and remind yourself almost every day what you genuinely want or need. You become goal-oriented just by imagining your outcomes and results. Your brain tends to provide you with every possible option of opportunity you can have by visualizing. By this, you can take your dreams and desire into the real world and achieve them by knowing the possible outcome already.

Everyone today wants their picture-perfect life. They are derived from working for it, and they even manage to achieve it sometimes. People love the success which they had already estimated to happen one day. They knew they would be successful because they not only worked for it but, they also visualized it in their brains. Everything eventually falls into place once you remind yourself of your goals constantly and sometimes write it into a few words. Writing your goals down helps you immensely. It is the idea of a constant reminder for you. So, now whenever you look on that paper or note, you find yourself recognizing your path towards success. That is one of the ways you could visualize yourself as a successful person in the coming era.

Another way to visualize your success is through private dialogue. One has to talk its way through success. It's a meaningful way to know your heart's content and what it is you are looking for in this whole dilemma. You can then easily interpret your thoughts into words. It becomes easier to tell people what you want. It is an essential factor to choose between something. Weighing your options, analyzing every detail, and you get your answer. It requires planning for every big event ahead and those to come. You ready yourself for such things beforehand so that you will know the result.

Every single goal of yours will count. So, we have to make sure that we give our attention to short-term goals and long-term goals. We have to take in the details, not leaving anything behind in the way or so. We have to make sure that everything we do is considered by ourselves first. Short-term goals are necessary for you to achieve small incomes, giving you a sense of pride. Long-term plans are more time-consuming, and it takes a lot of hard work and patience from a person. Visualizing a long-term goal might be a risk, something as big as a long-term achievement can have loads of different outcomes, and we may get distracted from our goal to become successful in life. But, visualizing does help you work correctly to get to know what will be your next step. You can make schemes in your mind about specific projects and how to work them out. Those scheming will help you in your present and future. So, it is essential to look at every small detail and imagine short-term goals and long-term goals.

Visualizing your success creates creative ideas in your mind. Your mind gets used to imagining things like these, and it automatically processes the whole plan in your mind. You then start to get more ideas and opportunities in life. You just need to close your eyes and imagine whatever you need to in as vivid detail as possible. Almost everything done by you is a result of thoughts of your mind. It is like another person living inside of you, who tells you what to do. It asks you to be alert and move. It also means the result of the possible outcome of a situation. Every action of you is your mind. Every word you speak is your mind talking.

Chapter 3:

8 Habits You Should Have For Life

The key to being happy, feeling energized, and having a productive life relies on a cycle of good habits. Achieving a state of spiritual and physical satisfaction is a conscious choice that you can make for yourself. Realize what attaining the greatest happiness means for you and strive to be as productive as you can to achieve that happiness. Work towards a sense of self-realization and start reaching for your goals one step at a time. Accomplishing this requires you to be confident and have a sense of self, built entirely on good habits. This includes having good attitudes, thoughts, and decision-making skills. Quoting the all-time favorite Poet-Maya Angelou, "a good life is achieved by liking who you are, what you do, and how you do it."

How do you put this in place? Living by good habits and discipline nourishes your potential and make you a better person in your surroundings.

Here are 8 habits you should adopt for life:

1. Create a clear Morning Routine That Is Non-Negotiable.

Creating a morning routine that you like and living up to it is essential. Before you start your day, you can turn to what you like doing be it running, meditating, or having a peaceful meal-time at breakfast. Whatever activities you choose based on your liking, kick start your day with that habit. Managing your morning routine and making it a habit enables you to start your day on a proactive and positive note. This will also help you in enhancing your mental health and productivity. Through trial and error find out what works best for you and stick to you day in and out.

2. Make a Point of Physically Exercising Your Body Muscles.

To jog your cognitive skills, relieve stress that has a hold on your performance stamina means that you need to exercise-go to the gym regularly or as much as you can. Do you still need more convincing reasons for hitting the gym? Here you go! Physical exercises increase your 'happy' moods chemically and propels the release of hormone endorphins. This hormone aids in getting rid of all the body and mind anxious feelings, hence enabling you to calm down.

3. Develop Quality Personal Relationships With Loved Ones.

The Harvard study of adult development has found that most of the existing long-term happiness for an individual is predicted through healthy relationships. Developing and maintaining close relationships with your loved ones or those close to people you consider family has been found to help someone live a longer and quality life. Hence it is the connections within your surroundings that make your life worthwhile.

4. Master an Attitude of Listening.

If you want to cultivate relationships in your life, be it professional or personal, communication is key. While communicating with your peers, family, or colleagues, you need to understand that listening to what they are saying is important. This is because you cannot have effective communication if it's one-sided. Remember that it is always important to value what others have to say. Their perspective might impact you, but most importantly, when you listen, you make others feel valued. Always try to understand the other party's point of view even if it defers from yours. Be open-minded to differing opinions. The more you listen, the more you get to learn.

5. Choose Natural Food Rather Than Processed Ones To Help Keep Your Brain Intact.

Whatever we eat always impacts our health, energy, moods, and concentration level. Whether you have weight issues or not, eating a healthy diet is essential. First off, the normality of having a healthy breakfast, lunch, or dinner is an act of practicing self-esteem and self-love. Therefore, eating healthy will always boost your self-esteem, lessen emotional issues, and your daily productivity will eventually be taken care of. If you choose to put unhealthy food in your body, you are not protecting the sanctuary that is giving you life. Make a conscious effort tot choose foods that give you the best chance of success, health, and wellness. As we all know, money can't buy health.

6. Be Appreciative More Than You Are Disparaging

Mastering the art of gratitude is a great way to live a happy, stress-free, healthy, and fulfilling life. As French writer Alphonse said: "We can complain because rose plants have thorns or we can rejoice as thorns also have roses." It's always easy to forget how fortunate you are while trying to push through life and the obstacles that come along with it. How do you master this art? Start a journal of appreciation to be grateful for the things you have. Take the time to appreciate those closest to you, those who care about you, and remember at least one good thing about yourself each and every day. Don't forget to make a note of what you have accomplished as well before you go to bed. The more you take notice of the little joys in life, the happier you will be.

7. Be With a Circle of Friends That Are Positive Minded.

Be careful about who you spend your precious time and energy with. A happy life can be contagious if we know where to attract it. Coincidentally, happiness is also the easiest way to develop positivity in our lives. With that in mind, choose to surround yourself which such people who will bring light into your world. Spend time with those who will nurture you each step of the way and don't hesitate to let go of the people who are eating away at your energy and spirits. Let's not forget the wise words of entrepreneur Jim Rohn, "You are the five people you spent the most time averagely. You only live once! Let it be worthwhile.

8. Take Breaks Regularly To Invest in Self-Care.

Although you might be very passionate about your work and your daily schedules, it is okay to take some time - an hour, minute, second, or even a day off. If you take a while to unwind, you will do wonderful things for your mood, mind, and self-esteem. Spend some time doing at least one thing that makes you feel good every day – whether it be listening to music, engaging in sports, starting a new hobby, dabbling in the arts, or even simply preparing a pleasant meal for yourself, you deserve to do it. Whatever floats your boat, don't neglect it!

Conclusion

Determination, persistence, and continuous effort are essential for the development of these habits. It can take just a few weeks or maybe more than a year to develop your habits, so long as you don't stop. It does not matter how long it takes.

What are you waiting for? Pull up your socks; it's your time to win at life.

Chapter 4:

7 Ways To Cultivate Emotions That Will Lead You To Greatness

Billions of men and women have walked the earth but only a handful have made their names engraved in history forever. These handful of people have achieved 'greatness' owing to their outstanding work, their passion and their character.

Now, greatness doesn't come overnight—greatness is not something you can just reach out and grab. Greatness is the result of how you have lived your entire life and what you have achieved in your lifetime. Against all your given circumstances, how impactful your life has been in this world, how much value you have given to the people around you, how much difference your presence has made in history counts towards how great you are. However, even though human greatness is subjective, people who are different and who have stood out from everyone else in a particular matter are perceived as great.

However, cultivating greatness in life asks for a 'great' deal of effort and all kinds of human effort are influenced by human emotions. So it's safe to say that greatness is, in fact, controlled by our emotions. Having said that, let's see what emotions are associated with greatness and how to cultivate them in real life:

1. Foster Gratitude

You cannot commence your journey towards greatness without being grateful first. That's right, being satisfied with what you already have in life and expressing due gratitude towards it will be your first step towards greatness. Being in a gratified emotional state at most times (if not all) will enhance your mental stability which will consequently help you perceive life in a different—or better point of view. This enhanced perception of life will remove your stresses and allow you to develop beyond the mediocrity of life and towards greatness.

2. Be As Curious As Child

Childhood is the time when a person starts to learn whatever that is around them. A child never stops questioning, a child never runs away from what they have to face. They just deal with things head on. Such kind of eagerness for life is something that most of us lose at the expense of time. As we grow up—as we know more, our interest keeps diminishing. We stop questioning anymore and accept what is. Eventually, we become entrapped into the ordinary. On the contrary, if we greet everything in life with bold eagerness, we expose ourselves to opportunities. And opportunities lead to greatness.

3. Ignite Your Passion

Passion has become a cliché term in any discussion related to achievements and life. Nevertheless, there is no way of denying the role of passion in driving your life force. Your ultimate zeal and fervor towards what you want in life is what distinguishes you to be great. Because admittedly, many people may want the same thing in life but how bad they want it—the intensity of wanting something is what drives people to stand out from the rest and win it over.

4. Become As Persistent As A Mountain

There are two types of great people on earth—1) Those who are born great and 2) Those who persistently work hard to become great. If you're reading this article, you probably belong to the later criteria. Being such, your determination is a key factor towards becoming great. Let nothing obstruct you—remain as firm as a mountain through all thick and thin. That kind of determination is what makes extraordinary out of the ordinary.

5. Develop Adaptability

As I have mentioned earlier, unless you are born great, your journey towards greatness will be an extremely demanding one. You will have to embrace great lengths beyond your comfort. In order to come out successful in such a journey, make sure that you become flexible to unexpected changes in your surroundings. Again, making yourself adaptable first in another journey in itself. You can't make yourself fit in adverse situations immediately. Adaptability or flexibility is cultivated prudently, with time, exposing yourself to adversities, little by little.

6. Confidence Is Key

Road to greatness often means that you have to tread a path that is discouraged by most. It's obvious—by definition, everybody cannot be great. People will most likely advise against you when you aspire something out of the ordinary. Some will even present logical explanations against you;especially your close ones. But nothing should waver your faith. You must remain boldly confident towards what you're pursuing. Only you can bring your greatness. Believe that.

7. Sense of Fulfilment Through Contributions

Honestly, there can be no greater feeling than what you'd feel after your presence has made a real impact on this world. If not, what else do we live for? Having contributed to the world and the people around you; this is the purpose of life. All the big and small contributions you make give meaning to your existence. It connects you to others, man and animal alike. It fulfills your purpose as a human being. We live for this sense of fulfillment and so, become a serial contributor. Create in yourself a greed for this feeling. At the end of the day, those who benefit from your contributions will revere you as great. No amount of success can be compared with this kind of greatness. So, never miss the opportunity of doing a good deed, no matter how minuscule or enormous.

In conclusion, these emotions don't come spontaneously. You have to create these emotions, cultivate them. And to cultivate these emotions, you must first understand yourself and your goals. With your eye on the prize, you have to create these emotions in you which will pave the path to your greatness. Gratitude, curiosity, passion, persistence, adaptability and fulfillment—each has its own weight and with all the emotions at play, nothing can stop you from becoming great in the truest form.

Chapter 5:

You Are Going To Be Successful

If you're listening to this ,

chances are you are going to be successful.

Not because this speech is remarkable

or contains information that will definitely change your life.

More because you have begun to do what

less than 20 percent of the population do.

You have begun to look for answers on how to improve your life.

Whether you find that right now

during this speech or in 6 moths from another,

or from a book or video.

If you persist you will find your answers,

and if applied, become successful.

It all depend on the action you take, but as always in life,

you are in control of everything - your thoughts and actions included.

You are infinitely more powerful than you currently believe.

You have capabilities in computing information

that even today's advanced technology doesn't come close to.

You know things that you don't know you know.

Many of your answers will come from inside you.

You beat the odds of 1 in 140 billion just to be born.

You were born as a defenceless baby that could not walk, talk or even chew food.

But you have evolved into a powerful soul capable of enacting change on a global scale if you just put your mind to it.

In your life you have learned countless bits of information.

You can be successful if you don't quit.

If you can take it, you can make it.

Take more than you currently believe.

You will make it, and then make it to something bigger than you can yet comprehend.

You will make it through with belief, persistence, and faith, just as with every powerful figure of history that has impacted the world before you.

Every major human achievement in history starts with one person.

It starts with one dream.

The people who are closest to you will probably doubt you.

They probably tell you that it is a pipe dream and that you should get a normal job and accept your life as it is.

Take everything they say with a pinch of salt.

They might be trying to protect you from disappointment but you know better.

You know the ultimate disappointment would be never trying and never following your dreams.
You know you can do more, have more, and help more.

To those with a vision, doing anything that doesn't contribute to that vision is a waste of time.
Don't let anyone tell you that you can't do something.
If you have that vision you are built to do this.
You shall not and will not accept anything less.

Bet on yourself because someone else's opinion
of you does not have to become your reality.
If you can believe in your success see it and feel
it as if it is real now.
It will not be long before it becomes so.

See it in your mind, believe, and feel it in your heart.
Set out in confidence from the start.
No matter the setbacks or failures,
never quit, and never admit defeat.

Get back on your feet and dust off your shoulder
because it is not over until you succeed or choose to give up.
The choice is yours, and always has been.
You are capable of climbing any mountain if you keep walking despite of
the altitude and bad weather on the way to the top.

Chapter 6:

10 Habits That Make You More Attractive

Being attractive does not necessarily connote physical appearance. More than the physical appearance, attraction renders the mental, emotional, and spiritual energy irresistible to others. Some people radiate with their energy and confidence regardless of whether they have money, looks, or are socially connected. These people are just irresistible, and you will find that people will always approach them for advice, help, or even long-term companionships. What makes them more attractive? Their sense of self-worth is always from within their souls as contrasted with how they look from outside. They don't seek validation from others- but find it within themselves.

However, this is not genetically connected, but a habit that we can build within ourselves. You need to pursue and maintain such habits for the benefit of a greater you.

Here are 10 habits that make you more attractive:

1. Connect With People More Deeply.

Attractive people are always likable people, and being likable is a skill. Being likable means that you should be interested in hearing others out rather than spending all the time thinking and talking about yourself. As entrepreneur Jim Rohn puts it- "Irresistible or likeable people possess an authentic personality that enables them to concentrate more on those around them." This requires that you are in most cases over yourself, meaning that you don't spend more time only thinking about yourself.

To have this habit going on in you, try to take conversations seriously. Put that phone down and listen! Learn what those around you are into - Ask questions, enquire about their dreams, fears, preferences, and views on life. Focus on what is being said rather than what the response is or what impact that might have on you. Always aim to make others everyone feel valued and important.

2. Treat Everyone With Respect.

Being polite and unfailingly respectful is the key to being likable. If you are always rude to others, you will find that over time people will tend to avoid you. You should strive to not only be respectful to someone you know and like, but also to strangers that you come across with. Attractive people treat everyone with the same respect they deserve bearing in mind that no one is better.

3. Follow the Platinum Rule.

The commonly known version of the golden rule is that you should treat others the same way you want them to treat you. This comes with a major flaw: the assumption that everyone aspires to be treated similarly. The rule ignores the fact people are different and are motivated differently. For instance, one person's love for public attention is another's person's execrate. However, you can opt for this flaw by adopting the platinum rule instead. The notion is that you should only treat others as they want to be treated. Attractive people are good at reading others and quickly adjust to their style and behavior, and as a result, they can treat them in a way that makes them feel comfortable.

4. Don't Try Too Hard To Put an Impression.

Attractive people who are easily likable don't try too hard to impress. Liking someone comes naturally, and it depends on their personality. Hence if you spend most of the time bragging about your success or smartness, you are simply harming yourself without knowing it. People who try too hard to be liked are not likable at all. Instead they come across as narcissistic and arrogant. If you wish to be an attractive person choose to be humble and down-to-earth instead. People will see your worth with their own two eyes.

5. Forgive and Learn From Your Mistakes.

Learning from our mistakes is synonymous with self-improvement. It is proven that psychological traits are essential in human mating or relationships, meaning that both intelligence and kindness are key. Being intelligent, in this case, doesn't necessarily mean the PHDs or Degrees.

It means that a person can demonstrate intelligence by learning from mistakes they make and handling the same well. You demonstrate this also by being kind to yourself whenever you make a mistake and avoiding the same mistake in the future. Attractive people know how to not take themselves too seriously and to have a laugh at themselves once in a while.

6. Smile Often

People tend to bond unconsciously with the body language portrayed while conversing. If you are geared towards making people more attracted to you, smile at them when conversing or talking to them. A smile makes other people feel comfortable in conversations, and in turn, they do the same to you. The feeling is remarkably good!

7. Likable People Are Authentic and Are Persons of Integrity.

People are highly attractive to realness. Attractive people portray who they are. Nobody has to expend energy or brainpower guessing their objective or predicting what they'll do next. They do this because they understand that no one likes a fake. People will gravitate toward you if you are genuine because it is easy to rely on you. On the flip side, it is also easy to resist getting close to someone if you don't know who they really are or how they actually feel.

People with high integrity are desirable because they walk their talk. Integrity is a straightforward idea, but it isn't easy to put into action. To show honesty every day, attractive people follow through with this trait. They refrain from gossiping about others and they do the right thing even if it hurts them to do so.

8. Recognize and Differentiate Facts and Opinions

Attractive people can deal gracefully and equally with divisive subjects and touchy issues. They don't shy away from expressing their views, but they clarify that they are just that: opinions, not facts. So, whenever you in a heated discussion, be it on politics or other areas with your peers, it is important to understand that people are different and are just as intelligent as you are. Everyone holds a different opinion; while facts always remain facts. Do not confuse the two to be the same.

9. Take Great Pleasure in The Little Things

Choose joy and gratitude in every moment – No matter if you are feeling sad, fearful, or happy. People who appreciates life for its up and downs will always appear attractive to others. Choose to see life as amazing and carefully approach it with joy and gratitude – Spread positive vibes and attract others to you that are also positive in nature. View obstacles as temporary, not inescapable. Everyone has problems, but it is how you deal with it each day that is important here. Optimistic people will always come out on top.

10. Treating friendships with priority

True friendships are a treasure. When you take your time and energy to nourish true friendships, you will naturally develop others skills necessary to sustain all forms of relationships in your life. People will always gravitate to a person who is genuinely friendly and caring. They want to be a part of this person's life because it brings them support and joy. Take these friendships with you to the distance.

Bonus Tip: Do Your Best to Look Good.

There is a huge difference between presentation and vanity. An attractive person will always make efforts to look presentable to others. This is comparable to tidying up the house before you receive visitors - which is a sign of gratitude to others. Don't show up sloppily to meetups and parties; this will give others the impression that you don't care about how you look which may put off others from approaching you. Always try your best in every situation.

Conclusion: Bringing it all in

Attractive people don't get these habits simply floating over their beds. They have mastered those attractive characteristics and behaviors consciously or subconsciously - which anyone can easily adopt.

You have to think about other people more than you think about yourself, and you have to make others feel liked, appreciated, understood, and seen. Note, the more you concentrate on others, the more attractive you will appear and become without even trying.

Chapter 7:

How to Value Being Alone

Some people are naturally happy alone. But for others, being solo is a challenge. If you fall into the latter group, there are ways to become more comfortable with being alone (yes, even if you're a hardcore extrovert).

Regardless of how you feel about being alone, building a good relationship with yourself is a worthy investment. After all, you *do* spend quite a bit of time with yourself, so you might as well learn to enjoy it.

Being alone isn't the same as being lonely.

Before getting into the different ways to find happiness in being alone, it's important to untangle these two concepts: being alone and being lonely. While there's some overlap between them, they're completely different concepts. Maybe you're a person who basks in solitude. You're not antisocial, friendless, or loveless. You're just quite content with alone time. You look forward to it. That's simply being alone, not being lonely.

On the other hand, maybe you're surrounded by family and friends but not relating beyond a surface level, which has you feeling empty and disconnected. Or maybe being alone just leaves you sad and longing for company. That's loneliness.

Short-term tips to get you started

These tips are aimed at helping you get the ball rolling. They might not transform your life overnight, but they can help you get more comfortable with being alone.

Some of them may be exactly what you needed to hear. Others may not make sense to you. Use them as stepping-stones. Add to them and shape them along the way to suit your lifestyle and personality.

1. **Avoid comparing yourself to others.**

This is easier said than done, but try to avoid comparing your social life to anyone else's. It's not the number of friends you have or the frequency of your social outings that matters. It's what works for you.

Remember, you have no way of knowing if someone with many friends and a stuffed social calendar is happy.

2. **Take a step back from social media.**

Social media isn't inherently bad or problematic, but if scrolling through your feeds makes you feel left out and stresses, take a few steps back. That feed doesn't tell the whole story. Not by a long shot.

You have no idea if those people are truly happy or just giving the impression that they are. Either way, it's no reflection on you. So, take a <u>deep breath</u> and put it in perspective.

Perform a test run and ban yourself from social media for 48 hours. If that makes a difference, try giving yourself a daily limit of 10 to 15 minutes and stick to it.

Don't be afraid to ask for help.

Sometimes, all the self-care, exercise, and gratitude lists in the world aren't enough to shake feelings of sadness or loneliness.

Consider reaching out to a therapist if:

- You're overly <u>stressed</u> and finding it difficult to cope.

- You have <u>symptoms of anxiety</u>.

- You have <u>symptoms of depression</u>.

You don't have to wait for a crisis point to get into <u>therapy</u>. Simply wanting to get better and spending time alone is a perfectly good reason to make an appointment.

Chapter 8:

How To Avoid The Hidden Danger of Comparing Yourself To Others.

"Everybody is a genius. But if you judge a fish by its ability to climb a tree, it will live its whole life believing that it is stupid." - Albert Einstein.

Comparing yourself to others allows them to drive your behavior. We tend to compare ourselves with people over several things. It could either be something genetic, like wishing to be taller or having a deeper voice. Or something that the other person naturally does well, but we envy them since we cannot achieve their level of perfection. Sometimes the comparison can be motivating, but a lot of the time, it's destructive.

You can be anything, but you can never be everything. When we compare ourselves to others, we often compare their best features against our average ones. For example, we try to play an instrument with our left hand while being right-handed, just because Sally at work plays it well like this. The unconscious realization that we are not naturally better than them often becomes self-destructive. But we have to understand that there's only one thing we're better at than all the other people; being ourselves. This is the only game we can win.

Life is all about becoming a better version of yourself every day. The moment we start with this mindset, the world around us starts to look better again. No longer do we have to stand relative to others when our only focus and energy is placed on what we're capable of now and how to improve ourselves. By putting our effort and energy into upgrading our operating system every day, we would become happier and free from all the shackles of false comparisons. Our focus would only be on the present moment. The only person you should compare yourself to is yourself, who you were yesterday and grew into today. The way people look at you is the same way you look at people, through a distorted lens shaped by experiences and expectations. But know that you don't owe anyone anything. It would help if you only strived to work on yourself and improve yourself.

Stop comparing yourself with people and focus internally; you will start better at what matters to you. It might sound simple, but it's not easy. Play your own game instead of stealing someone else's scoreboard. Find comfort in knowing that someone will always be less than you in things you're good at. Don't steal away your happiness by comparing yourself with others. As Theodore Roosevelt once said, "Comparison is the thief of joy." You are so much more capable than you think, so don't strip off this joy from yourself. You are unique and amazing on your own!

Chapter 9:

Happy People Use Their Character Strengths

One of the most popular exercises in the science of positive psychology (some argue it is the single most popular exercise) is referred to as "use your signature strengths in new ways." But what does this exercise mean? How do you make the most of it to benefit yourself and others?

On the surface, the exercise is self-explanatory:

a. Select one of your highest strengths – one of your **character strengths** that is core to who you are, is easy for you to use, and gives you energy;

b. Consider a new way to express the strength each day;

c. Express the strength in a new way each day for at least 1 week.

Studies repeatedly show that this exercise is connected with long-term benefits (e.g., 6 months) such as higher levels of happiness and lower levels of depression.

PUT THE EXERCISE INTO PRACTICE

In practice, however, people sometimes find it surprisingly challenging to come up with new ways to use one of their signature strengths. This is because we are very accustomed to using our strengths. We frequently use our strengths mindlessly without much awareness. For example, have you paid much attention to your use of self-regulation as you brush your teeth? Your level of prudence or kindness while driving? Your humility while at a team meeting?

For some strengths, it is easy to come up with examples. Want to apply **curiosity** in a new way? Below is a sample mapping of what you might do. Keep it simple. Make it complex. It's up to you!

- On Monday, take a new route home from work and explore your environment as you drive.
- On Tuesday, ask one of your co-workers a question you have not previously asked them.
- On Wednesday, try a new food for lunch – something that piques your curiosity to taste.
- On Thursday, call a family member and explore their feelings about a recent positive experience they had.
- On Friday, take the stairs instead of the elevator and explore the environment as you do.
- On Saturday, as you do one household chore (e.g., washing the dishes, vacuuming), pay attention to 3 novel features of the activity while you do it. Example: Notice the whirring sound of the vacuum, the accumulation of dust swirling around in the container, the warmth of the water as you wash the dishes, the sensation of the weight of a single plate or cup, and so on.
- On Sunday, ask yourself 2 questions you want to explore about yourself – reflect or journal your immediate responses.
- Next Monday….keep going!

WIDENING THE SCOPE

In some instances, you might feel challenged to come up with examples. Let me help. After you choose one of your signature strengths, consider the following 10 areas to help jolt new ideas within you and stretch your approach to the strength.

How might I express the character strength...

- At work
- In my closest relationship
- While I engage in a hobby
- When with my friends
- When with my parents or children
- When I am alone at home
- When I am on a team
- As the leader of a project or group
- While I am driving
- While I am eating

Chapter 10:

5 Ways Quitting Something Can Bring You Joy

Do you ever wonder if you will ever be truly happy in your life? Do you wonder if happiness is just a hoax and success is an illusion? Do you feel like they don't exist? I know a friend who felt like this a little while ago. At the time, she was making a six-figure income, was working for her dream company (Apple), and had a flexible work schedule. Despite all this, she was miserable. She would have never been able to quit my job if not for the practice she got from quitting little things.

Of all the things that she tried, quitting these seven little things made her the happiest.

1. Quit Reading the News

News headlines are usually about happenings around the world. Most times, they are negative. Negative headlines make for better stories than positive headlines. Would you read a headline that says 'Electric Chair Makes a Comeback' or a headline that says 'Legislation debate in Tennessee'? See what I mean.

Journalists have to write stories that interest us. I can't blame them for that. Changing the time that I caught up on the news helped me be more positive during the day. Start reading inspirational posts first thing in the morning instead of news. You can still catch the news later, around 11 am instead of at 6 am.

2. Quit Hunching Your Shoulders

This boosted my confidence levels.

We hunch our shoulders and take up as little space as possible when we feel nervous and not too comfortable. This is body language 101.

Keeping a posture, opening up your shoulders will make you feel more confident during the day. But, I must admit it will make you more tired than usual. It will take you at least a total of 45 days before you start doing this effortlessly.

3. Quit Keeping a Corporate Face at Work

We are all trained not to show real feelings at work. Having a corporate face is good for corporate, not for you. Smiling all day, even when you are upset, will lift your mood. It will make you feel better sooner. Studies have shown that smiling makes you happy.

4. Quit Writing Huge Goals

It is better to write and work towards achievable goals before starting to write our stretch goals. Stretch goals are great to push ourselves. But, we all need achievable goals to boost confidence and to have successes that we can build momentum on. This can be hard for you if you are an overachiever.

5. Quit Eating Fries and Eat Oranges Instead

Fries are comfort food for a lot of people. But eating them saps energy.

Eat oranges instead of fries every time you feel down and feel the need for comfort food. This not only boosts your energy but will also help you lose some pounds if you want to. Plus, this will give you energy and clarity of mind.

Chapter 11:

10 Habits of Jennifer Lawrence

Jennifer Lawrence is one of Hollywood's most famous actress, thanks to her role in films such as "The Hunger Games" and "Silver Linings Playbook." But, before her tremendous success, Lawrence struggled to build a name for herself as an actress and model in New York, where she moved when she was 14 years old. After breaking out as the tough-as-nails teenager Ree in the 2010 indie drama "Winter's Bone," Lawrence went on to star in multiple "X-Men" films and drama such as "American Hustle."

I can't think of anyone who doesn't adore Jennifer Lawrence. What is it about this actress that makes her so appealing? It's easy to list a thousand reasons to admire Jennifer Lawrence -from her incredible skill to her quick-witted humour- but honestly, the life lessons she attracts everyone to her.

Here are 10 life habits that Lawrence offers as lessons simply by being herself.

1. Strive for Health and Strength

"I'm never going to starve myself for a part," she declared on the cover of Elle in December 2012. "I don't want little girls to think, 'Oh, I want to look like Katniss; hence I'll skip meals." When you're trying to get your physique to appear just suitable, Emma on the other end is trying to make her body appear muscular and robust rather than skinny.

2. Refresh Yourself

How many times has Lawrence stumbled? That's what probably comes to your mind every time you see her trip over the hem of her gown at an awards presentation. Can anyone blame the girl for this? Those outfits appear to be impossible to walk in! But she trips, and every time, without fail, she gets back up and continues walking.

3. Accept Responsibility for Your Mistakes

Lawrence's awkward moments are all the more endearing because she is always the first to laugh at how clumsy she is when she stands. Remember when she collapsed at the 2013 Academy Awards? Or when she collapsed on the red carpet of the 2014 Academy Awards? What does it matter? We're all human, and J. Law never tries to hide it by acting cool and so should you.

4. The Truth Will Set You Free

Even if your truth seems to hurt more, such as that you pee very quickly or that your breasts are unequal, J. Law says that it is what it is, and to be anything other than herself isn't allowed. Embrace your flaws!

5. Look Past the Hype

Remember to key in what's genuine and what's not, and to keep your things in perspective, look past those who take themselves too seriously.

6. Maintain An Open Mind

Lawrence told E! News that her acting job will not bind her for the rest of her life. However, she understands that things happen and that people's lives change, and she is prepared to keep an open mind about it. Being open-minded will direct you to break the monotony for future possibilities.

7. Nobody Is Flawless

Can you recall a scene in American Hustle in which Lawrence's character discusses nail polish? Do you remember the nail polish? She claims it's the smell that keeps drawing her back since it's delicious on the outside but rotten on the inside. Not only is it a beautiful moment, but the discussion is a metaphor for everyone's good and evil sides. Nobody is flawless, and no one loves it when others claim to be.

8. Humility

During a BBC Radio 1 interview, Lawrence remarked her involvement in "The Hunger Games," where she genuinely adores watching the movies she makes because she gets to see how much of a troll, bad, and untalented is. Weird! Indeed, you wouldn't agree with her right? Bu she's adorable because she is humble.

9. Maintain a Sense of Humour

During an interview with Vogue, Lawrence sense of humour could be seen when she cracked a joke on how seeing 13-year olds give her nightmares. She effortlessly doesn't take life too seriously.

10. Love Your Body

Lawrence has spoken out numerous times about her body, challenging unrealistic beauty standards. She claimed in an interview with FLARE magazine that she would rather appear overweight on camera (and appear normal) than diet only to dress like a scarecrow. That is a whole lot of body positivity just for you!

Conclusion

Jennifer will teach you profound truths- when she acts, and when she put on a mask that conceals who she truly is. She given up none of her power by leaving the covers on the screen and refusing to act to "fit in" with Hollywood culture.

Chapter 12:

8 Habits That Can Make You Happy

We're always striving for something, whether it's a promotion, a new truck, or anything else. This brings us to an assumption that "when this happens, You'll finally be happy."

While these important events ultimately make us happy, research suggests that this pleasure does not last. A Northwestern University study compared the happiness levels of ordinary people to those who had won the massive lottery in the previous years. It was found that the happiness scores of both groups were nearly equal.

The false belief that significant life events determine your happiness or sorrow is so widespread that psychologists have given it a name- "impact bias." The truth is that event-based happiness is transitory. Satisfaction is artificial; either create it or not. Long-term happiness is achieved through several habits. Happy people develop behaviors that keep them satisfied daily.

Here are eight habits that can make you happy.

1. Take Pride in Life's Little Pleasures.

We are prone to falling into routines by nature. This is, in some ways, a positive thing. It helps conserve brainpower while also providing comfort. However, it is possible to be so engrossed in your routine that you neglect to enjoy the little pleasures in life. Happy people understand the value of savoring the taste of their meal, revel in a great discussion they just had, or even simply stepping outside to take a big breath of fresh air.

2. Make Efforts To Be Happy.

Nobody, not even the most ecstatically happy people, wakes up every day feeling this way. They work harder than everyone else. They understand how easy it is to fall into a routine where you don't check your emotions or actively strive to be happy and optimistic. People who are happy continually assess their moods and make decisions with their happiness in mind.

3. Help other people.

Helping others not only makes them happy, but it also makes you happy. Helping others creates a surge of dopamine, oxytocin, and serotonin, all of which generate pleasant sensations. According to Harvard research, people who assist others are ten times more likely to be focused at work and 40% more likely to be promoted. According to the same study, individuals who constantly provide social support are the most likely to be happy during stressful situations. As long as you don't overcommit yourself, helping others will positively affect your mood.

4. Have Deep Conversations.

Happy people understand that happiness and substance go hand in hand. They avoid gossip, trivial conversation, and passing judgment on others. Instead, they emphasize meaningful interactions. You should interact with others on a deeper level because it makes you feel good, creates emotional connections, and, importantly, it's an intriguing way to learn.

5. Get Enough Sleep.

I've pounded this one too hard over the years, and I can't emphasize enough how important sleep is for enhancing your attitude, focus, and self-control. When you sleep, your brain recharges, removing harmful proteins that accumulate as byproducts of regular neuronal activity during the day. This guarantees that you awaken alert and focused. When you don't get enough quality sleep, your energy, attention, and memory all suffer. Even in the absence of a stressor, sleep loss elevates stress hormone levels. Sleep is vital to happy individuals because it makes them feel good, and they know how bad they feel when they don't get enough sleep.

6. Surround yourself with the right people

Happiness is contagious; it spreads through people. Surrounding yourself with happy people boosts your confidence, encourages your creativity, and is simply enjoyable.

Spending time with negative people has the opposite effect. They get others to join their self-pity party so that they may feel better about themselves. Consider this: if someone was smoking, would you sit there all afternoon inhaling the second-hand smoke? You'd step back, and you should do the same with negative people.

7. Always Stay Positive.

Everyone, even happy people, encounters difficulties daily. Instead of moaning about how things could or should have been, happy people think about what they are grateful for. Then they find the best approach to the situation, that is, dealing with it and moving on. Pessimism is a powerful source of sadness. Aside from the damaging effects on your mood, the problem with a pessimistic mindset is that it becomes a self-fulfilling prophecy. If you expect bad things, you are more likely to encounter horrific events. Gloomy thoughts are difficult to overcome unless you see how illogical they are. If you force yourself to look at the facts, you'll discover that things aren't nearly as awful as you think.

8. Maintain a Growth Mindset

People's core attitudes can be classified into two types: fixed mindsets and growth mindsets. You believe you are who you are and cannot change if you have a fixed attitude. When you are challenged, this causes problems because anything that looks to be more than you can handle will make you feel despondent and overwhelmed. People with a growth mindset believe that with effort, they can progress. They are happy as a result of their improved ability to deal with adversity. They also outperform those with a fixed perspective because they welcome difficulties and see them as chances to learn something new.

Conclusion

It can be tough to maintain happiness, but investing your energy in good habits will pay off. Adopting even a couple of the habits on this list will have a significant impact on your mood.

Chapter 13:

Don't Let Eating, Sleeping, and Working Out Get In The Way of Your Productivity

From the time of Man's descend on this planet, We have literally been eating, sleeping, and working for our basic requirements.

With time and population, we did invent some things which were perfected with time as well. But in general, when you leave your teenage or enter middle age, you get into this routine of chores that only keep the cycle of life running.

The things that we take for granted today, were considered magic only a couple of hundred years ago. The feats we have done in the last fifty years may be more important and revolutionary compared to all human history. But this hasn't stopped us from seeking more.

We have two basic requirements to live; We need air to breathe and we need food to fuel up the tank. But if we start to live our lives only for those two things alone, we are no better than a prehistoric caveman.

The purpose of life is far bigger than what we perceive today.

Yeah, sometimes we get into existential crisis because we never really know what our lives mean. What the future will be and can be? What will happen at the end of all this? What was our purpose all along?

These things are natural to every sane human perception and thinking. Some people spend all their lives in search of the true meaning, in search of the truth. But the truth is that you can never know even if you have all things planned with a foolproof sketch.

But what I can tell you is that no effort goes to waste if you have a true motive. We have come too far to give up on things and leave them for others to complete. We can be satisfied with living a simple life of straightforward tasks, but we can never be fully content with our lives.

Human nature dictates us to have a second look, a second thought on even the most obvious things around us. This habit of questioning everything has brought us out of the supernatural and made us achieve things that were not even in the realm of magic.

The biggest hunger a human mind can have is the hunger for knowledge. Human beings were meant to shape up the world for the better.

Human consciousness is so vast that its limits are still unknown. So why are we still stuck on the same habits and knowledge we were born with. Why can't we ask more questions? Why can't we try to find more answers?

The only way forward for us is to keep feeding ourselves more goals and more reasons to get busy.

Life isn't just about getting up in the morning. It is about finding our true potential. It is about finding easier ways to solve problems. It is about finding bigger, better, and greater things for the generations to come.

We were given this life to inspire and be inspired. But if we have nothing new to offer to at least ourselves, what purpose are we serving then?

Chapter 14:

5 Tips to Increase Your Attention Span

If you've ever found it difficult to get through a challenging task at work, studied for an important exam, or spent time on a finicky project, you might have wished you could increase your ability to concentrate.

Concentration refers to the mental effort you direct toward whatever you're working on or learning at the moment. It's sometimes confused with attention span, but attention span refers to the length of time you can concentrate on something.

If that sounds familiar, keep reading to learn more about research-backed methods to help improve your attention span. We'll also go over some conditions that can affect concentration and steps to take if trying to increase concentration on your own just doesn't seem to help.

1. Train Your Brain

Playing certain types of games can help you get better at concentrating. Try:

- sudoku

- crossword puzzles

- chess

- jigsaw puzzles

- word searches or scrambles

- memory games

Results of a 2015 study Trusted Source of 4,715 adults suggest spending 15 minutes a day, five days a week, on brain training activities can greatly impact concentration.

Brain training games can also help you develop your working and short-term memory, as well as your processing and problem-solving skills.

Older adults

The effects of brain training games may be particularly important for older adults since memory and concentration often tend to decline with age.

Research from 2014Trusted Source that looked at 2,832 older adults followed up on participants after ten years. Older adults who completed between 10 and 14 cognitive training sessions saw improved cognition, memory, and processing skills.

After ten years, most study participants reported they could complete daily activities at least as well as they could at the beginning of the trial, if not better.

2. Get Your Game On

Brain games may not be the only type of game that can help improve concentration. Newer research also suggests playing video games could help boost concentration.

A 2018 study looking at 29 people found evidence to suggest an hour of gaming could help improve visual selective attention (VSA). VSA refers to your ability to concentrate on a specific task while ignoring distractions around you.

Its small size limited this study, so these findings aren't conclusive. The study also didn't determine how long this increase in VSA lasted.

Study authors recommend future research continue exploring how video games can help increase brain activity and boost concentration.

3. Improve Sleep

Sleep deprivation can easily disrupt concentration, not to mention other cognitive functions, such as memory and attention.

Occasional sleep deprivation may not cause too many problems for you. But regularly failing to get a good night's sleep can affect your mood and performance at work.

Being too tired can even slow down your reflexes and affect your ability to drive or do other daily tasks.

A demanding schedule, health issues, and other factors sometimes make it difficult to get enough sleep. But it's important to try and get as close to the recommended amount as possible on most nights.

Many experts recommend adults aim for 7 to 8 hours of sleep each night.

4. Make Time For Exercise

Increased concentration is among the <u>many benefits</u> of regular exercise. Exercise benefits everyone. A <u>2018 study</u> looking at 116 fifth-graders found evidence to suggest daily physical activity could help improve both concentration and attention after just four weeks.

Another Source looking at older adults suggests that just a year of moderate aerobic physical activity can help stop or reverse memory loss that occurs with brain atrophy related to age.

Do what you can

Although aerobic exercise is recommended, doing what you can is better than doing nothing at all. Depending on your fitness and weight goals, you may want to exercise more or less.

But sometimes, it just isn't possible to get the recommended amount of exercise, especially if you live with physical or mental health challenges.

5. Spend Time In Nature

If you want to boost your concentration naturally, try to get outside every day, even for just 15 to 20 minutes. You might take a short walk through a park. Sitting in your garden or backyard can also help. Any natural environment has <u>benefits.</u>

Scientific evidence increasingly supports the positive impact of natural environments. Research from <u>2014</u>Trusted Source found evidence to suggest including plants in office spaces helped increase concentration and productivity and workplace satisfaction, and air quality.

Try adding a plant or two to your workspace or home for a range of <u>positive benefits</u>. Succulents make great choices for low-maintenance plants if you don't have a green thumb.

Chapter 15:

Happy People Spend Money on Experiences, Not Material Things

When we spend money on ourselves and the people we care about, we're likely doing more than simply buying things. Our ultimate goal is to create feelings of happiness, satisfaction, and well-being on a deeper level. [1]

But are we spending our money in the best ways to achieve those results? Many of us spend in ways that do little to help us get what we truly want. Researchers say that there is a relationship between how we spend money and happiness. Hence, the good news is that we have the opportunity to shift our spending patterns to help increase our happiness and help us create more meaningful lives. So, where do we begin?

Experiences Last

Our culture tells us that buying lots of stuff will make us happy. And that can be true, but only up to a point. Research published in the Journal of Positive Psychology reveals that people who spent money on experiences rather than on material goods were happier because the excitement we often get from purchasing things tends to diminish quickly as we get used to them and start taking them for granted. However, the joy and memories experiences bring can give us stronger feelings of satisfaction. That can be true even if the experience doesn't last nearly as long as the physical item we purchased.

Think of it this way: A material item like a car or a TV is an item that is separable from you. Experiences are more likely to become part of who you are as a person. Also, purchasing an item is often a solitary action, especially when buying online. When we participate in experiences with friends, family, co-workers, and others, those experiences may strengthen and enhance the most important relationships. Memories from shared experiences can later be recalled among the people who took part in them and told to others who weren't part of the experience.

Tips for Experiential Spending

So, what can you do to get the most out of your experiential spending?

Here are a couple of quick ideas:

1: Think smaller and more frequently. It's easy to think that only big and expensive experiences, such as a grand vacation every year or two, are the way to go. But, spending on smaller experiences more frequently may give you more satisfaction and bang for your buck.

2: Give gifts that enhance the experience. One key to getting the most pleasure and happiness from experience might be to give gifts that help facilitate meaningful experiences. For example, buying a better camera or binoculars to use during a unique outdoor travel experience or buying high-end sporting equipment for the family can lead to better outdoor experiences in a fun, interesting locations. Gifts that help create happy social experiences can be money very well spent.

Chapter 16:

Do More of What Already Works

In 2004, nine hospitals in Michigan began implementing a new procedure in their intensive care units (I.C.U.). Almost overnight, healthcare professionals were stunned by its success.

Three months after it began, the procedure had cut the infection rate of I.C.U. Patients by sixty-six percent. Within 18 months, this one method had saved 75 million dollars in healthcare expenses. Best of all, this single intervention saved the lives of more than 1,500 people in just a year and a half. The strategy was immediately published in a blockbuster paper for the <u>New England Journal of Medicine</u>.

This medical miracle was also simpler than you could ever imagine. It was a checklist.

This five-step checklist was the simple solution that Michigan hospitals used to save 1,500 lives. Think about that for a moment. There were no technical innovations. There were no pharmaceutical discoveries or cutting-edge procedures. The physicians just stopped skipping steps. They implemented the answers they already had on a more consistent basis.

New Solutions vs. Old Solutions

We tend to undervalue answers that we have already discovered. We underutilize old solutions—even best practices—because they seem like something we have already considered.

Here's the problem: *"Everybody already knows that"* is very different from *"Everybody already does that."* Just because a solution is known doesn't mean it is utilized.

Even more critical, just because a solution is implemented occasionally doesn't mean it is implemented consistently. Every physician knew the five steps on Peter Pronovost's checklist, but very few did all five steps flawlessly each time.

We assume that new solutions are needed to make real progress, but that isn't always the case. This pattern is just as present in our personal lives as it is in corporations and governments. We waste the resources and ideas at our fingertips because they don't seem new and exciting.

There are many examples of behaviors, big and small, that have the opportunity to drive progress in our lives if we just did them with more consistency—flossing every day—never missing workouts. Performing fundamental business tasks each day, not just when you have time— apologizing more often. Writing Thank You notes each week.

Of course, these answers are boring. Mastering the fundamentals isn't sexy, but it works. No matter what task you are working on, a simple checklist of steps you can follow right now—fundamentals that you have known about for years—can immediately yield results if you just practice them more consistently.

Progress often hides behind boring solutions and underused insights. You don't need more information. You don't need a better strategy. You just need to do more of what already works.

Chapter 17:

Happy People Are Proactive About Relationships

Researchers have found that as human beings we are only capable of maintaining up to 150 meaningful relationships, including five primary, close relationships.

This holds true even with the illusion of thousands of "friends" on social media platforms such as Facebook, Instagram, and Twitter. If you think carefully about your real interactions with people, you'll find the five close/150 extended relationships rule holds true.

Perhaps not coincidentally, Tony Robbins, the personal development expert, and others argue that your attitudes, behavior, and success in life are the sum total of your five closest relationships. So, toxic relationships, toxic life.

With this in mind, it's essential to continue to develop relationships that are positive and beneficial. **But in today's distracted world, these relationships won't just happen.**

We need to be proactive about developing our relationships.

My current favorite book on personal development is Tim Ferriss's excellent, though long, 700+ page book, *Tools of Titans: The Tactics, Routines, and Habits of Billionaires, Icons, and World-Class Performers*.

At one point, Ferriss quotes retired women's volleyball great Gabby Reece:

I always say that I'll go first.... That means if I'm checking out at the store, I'll say "hello" first. If I'm coming across somebody and make eye contact, I'll smile first. [I wish] people would experiment with that in their life a little bit: be first, because — not all times, but most times — it comes in your favor... The response is pretty amazing.... I was at the park the other day with the kids.

Oh, my God. Hurricane Harbor [water park]. It's like hell. There were these two women a little bit older than me. We couldn't be more different, right? And I walked by them, and I just looked at them and smiled. The smile came to their face so instantly. They're ready, but you have to go first because now we're being trained in this world [to opt out] — nobody's going first anymore.

Be proactive: start the conversation

I agree. I was excited to read this principle because I adopted this by default years ago, and it's given me the opportunity to hear the most amazing stories and develop the greatest relationships you can imagine.

On airplanes, in the grocery store, at lunch, I've started conversations that led to trading heartfelt stories, becoming friends, or doing business together. A relationship has to start someplace, and that can be any place in any moment.

Be proactive: lose your fear of being rejected

I also love this idea because it will help overcome one of the main issues I hear from my training and coaching clients – the fear of making an initial connection with someone they don't know.

This fear runs deep for many people and may be hardwired in humans. We are always observing strangers to determine if we can trust them – whether they have positive or dangerous intent.

In addition, **we fear rejection. Our usual negative self-talk says something like,** *If I start the conversation, if I make eye contact, if I smile, what if it's not returned?*

What if I'm rejected, embarrassed, or ignored by no response? I'll feel like an idiot, a needy loser.

Chapter 18:

8 Habits That Make People Dislike You

As human beings, we all have a deep innate need to be liked. It's very easy for someone to make a sweeping judgement based on their first impression of you. The vast majority believe that being likable is a matter of natural, inexplicable traits that only belong to a fortunate few; good looks, fierce social media, among others. The reality is that every detail matters; from your interpersonal skills, your last name, your smell, and so on. Generally speaking, certain behaviors make people hold back from liking you. Unless you get such habits done with, it's always easy to fall prey to the unlikeable discrepancy.

Here are 8 habits that makes people dislike you.

1. **Self-Indulgence**

On the top of the list is a self-centered person. If you are always talking about yourself, greedy, or simply just so full of it, it's not easy to understand why people will find you very annoying. If you are always bragging about your triumphs or lamenting about your problems, be prepared for people to avoid you. If the talk is just about you, and you always, you will be avoided at all costs. Focus on others and their problems instead of your own. Let them share their thoughts and ideas with you equally; that is the basic foundation of a conversation. Don't be full of yourself!

2. **Being Too Serious.**

People are drawn to enthusiastic individuals. However, because they are often absorbed in their work, enthusiastic people can become too serious or uninterested. This is a turn off as people will find you likable only when you take pride in work while paving way for fun moments too. Which means that you are serious with whatever you are doing but also cherish those socially fun times. This, in turn, demonstrates that the moments you share with others are just as important as your work.

3. **Narrow-Mindedness and Rigidity.**

When you are open-minded, you are easily likable and approachable. This is in contrast to rigidity and narrow-minded traits. When you are conversing with someone, you must be willing to accept all opinions that differ from yours, even if you don't always agree with them. You may not like what everyone has to say all the time, but it does not imply that you start picking fights and arguing about every small matter. An open-minded person is approachable and so likable. People can talk to you about anything because they know you will not be upset. They will not fear being judged by you because you portray a neutral aura.

If you go into a debate with preconceived views, you are unable to see things from someone else's perspective. It will lead to disputes and arguments. Nobody loves someone who is rigid and judgmental.

4. **Dishonesty and Emotional Manipulation**

One of the most typical traits of unlikable people is dishonesty. Everyone lies at some point in their lives, but people begin to avoid you when lying becomes a habit. You may lose good friends as a result of this tendency. Dishonest people are frequently manipulative. Instead of confessing their shortcomings, they would tell a lie to avoid an awkward scenario. They can concoct a thousand lies to conceal a single fact. If you engage in the habit of lying, people will quickly see your true colors and you may see your friends dropping like flies.

5. **You Are a Gossip Mogul.**

When people get carried away with gossiping, they make themselves look awful. Wallowing in gossip about other people's actions or misfortunes may end up hurting their feelings if the gossip reaches them. What's more, it's that gossip will always make you look unpleasant and bitter. People will associate you with as the person who goes around spreading rumors and misinformation to others. You may begin to be viewed as untrustworthy in other people's eyes and people will stop telling you things.

6. **A Name-Dropper.**

One of the most vexing hobbies of unlikable people is name-dropping. It is advantageous if you know a few influential and well-known people. Name-dropping in every conversation, on the other hand, will make you obnoxious and unlikable. Name-dropping is a characteristic of insecure persons who are always looking for attention. People will know who you are with without you having to mention it on every occasion. Nobody likes someone who always feels the need to appear superior or more important than others. Sure it'll be interesting to engage in conversations about these people you know, but do it wisely.

7. **You Are Constant Phone-Checker.**

Checking the phone while having a moment with someone is one of the worst habits of dislikeable people. It is just awful! You should opt out of it.

When you are alone, it is ok to look at your smartphone. However, continuously checking your phone while eating dinner with someone or attending a meeting is impolite. It implies that you are not paying attention to the person who is trying to have this conversation with you. Being addicted or glued to your phone all the time will give the impression that nothing is more important to you than your screen time. You will find that it turns people off and you may not get asked out for a meal again. Don't be so distracted. Pay attention to the person all the time.

8. **Sharing Too Much Information, Too Soon.**

Chatting up with others necessitates a decent standard of sharing; sharing too much about yourself straight away however, may be inappropriate. Take caution not to share personal concerns or admissions too early. Likable people allow the others to direct them when it is appropriate for them to open up. Oversharing might have an impression that you are self-centered and unconcerned about conversation balance. Consider this: if you dive into the details of your life without first learning about the other person, you're sending the impression that you consider them as nothing more than a sounding board for your troubles.

Conclusion

If you're still wondering why others dislike you, look again at the above signs and habits of unlikable people. Being likable has nothing to do with being gorgeous or intelligent! All you have to do is respect other people's time and opinions. When spending time with someone, you must pay close attention. Being open-minded, sensitive, and understanding automatically makes you likable. When you become more conscious of how other people perceive your behavior, you pave the route toward being more likable.

Chapter 19:

<u>Believe in Yourself</u>

Listen up. I want to tell you a story. This story is about a boy. A boy who became a man, despite all odds. You see, when he was a child, he didn't have a lot going for him. The smallest and weakest in his class, he had to struggle every day just to keep up with his peers. Every minute of every hour was a fight against an opponent bigger and stronger than he was - and every day he was knocked down. Beaten. Defeated. But... despite that... despite everything that was going against him... this small, weak boy had one thing that separated him from hundreds of millions of people in this world. A differentiating factor that made a difference in the matter of what makes a winner in this world of losers. You see this boy believed in himself. No matter the odds, he believed fundamentally that he had the power to overcome anything that got in his way! It didn't matter how many times he was knocked down, he got RIGHT BACK UP!

Now it wasn't easy. It hurt like hell. Every time he failed was another reminder of how far behind he was. A reminder of the nearly insurmountable gap between him and everyone else and lurking behind that reminder was the temptation, the suggestion to just give up. Throw in the towel. Surrender the win. Yet believe me when I tell you that no matter HOW tough things got, no matter HOW much he wanted to give in, a small voice in his heart keep saying... not today... just once more... I know it hurts but I can try again... Just. Once. More.

You see more than anything in this world HE KNEW that deep inside him was a greatness just WAITING to be tapped into! A power that most people would never see, but not him. It didn't matter what the world threw at him, because he'd be damned if he let his potential die alongside him. And all it took? All it required to unlock the chasm of greatness inside was a moment to realise the lies the world tried to tell him. In less than a second he recognised the light inside that would ignite a spark of success to address the ones who didn't believe that he could do it. The ones who told him to give up! Get out! Go home and roam the streets where failure meets those who weren't born to sit at the seat at the top!

Yet what they didn't know is that being born weak didn't matter any longer 'cause in his fight to succeed he became stronger. Rising up to the heights beyond, he WOULD NOT GIVE UP till he forged a bond within his heart that ensured NO MATTER THE ODDS, no matter what anyone said about him, no matter what the world told him, he had something that NO ONE could take away from him. A power so strong it transformed this boy into a man. A loser into a winner. A failure into a success. That, is the power of self-belief...

Chapter 20:

10 Habits of Meryl Streep

Meryl Streep is an American actress known for her incomparable abilities; she can adapt to complicated accents, sing, be a comedian, and play old male rabbi. Meryl roles have brought her from African bush and Greece beaches, Julia Child's legendary kitchen, and Disney wonderland. If you have watched Meryl ace her roles, this doesn't sound like a standard joke. Meryl is undoubtedly a Hollywood queen with 21 Academy Award nominations and three wins for Kramer vs. Kramer, Sophie's Choice, and The Iron Lady. Rising to such fame, staying modest and brilliant, and, ahem-an an estimation of $ 160 million net-worth, Meryl maintains specific principles.

Here are 10 habits of Meryl Streep to enumerate from.

1. Focus on the Skills Rather Than Looks

During an interview with Vogue, Meryl said that stressing about your weight or skin will derail you. Instead, concentrate on what you enjoy doing, as what you put your hands on should be your world. Meryl had repeatedly reiterated her stance on choosing genius over beauty, even when told she is "too ugly."

2. Focus on the Bigger Picture

It is natural for people to succumb to the muck of stress, deadlines, and anxiety. It is also common to find yourself overcommitting or doubting whether you can do a task or achieve a specific goal. However, if you take a step back and breathe, you will see the bigger picture. Meryl said that the one thing she could tell her 20-something old self would be to think big. She wished she could have devoted more time comprehending the critical role she had in society.

3. Be Authentic

Never, ever apologize for being true to yourself. Meryl was called fat, ugly, and her nose being ridiculed. She recalls how at first, her self-esteem declined to a point she couldn't even watch her shows but later made it her aim to criticize societal expectations of a slim, perfect, and beautiful goddess Hollywood queen.

4. Listen Always

Meryl studies accents as well as what they communicate to stay in tune with the roles she portrays. She achieves this by empathically listening. It means listening before and after work and in between work-to those you associate daily to learn, listening to everything.

5. Age Is Just a Number

Meryl insists on embracing your age and doing what you can utmost at any phase. She has always been vocal against Hollywood manifestations of stripping female actresses short. Meryl has used her influence to fight against ageism, demonstrating that women of all ages deserve to be heard, seen, and appreciated.

6. Start by Starting, Stay Consistent

In the 90s, Meryl kept on making moves despite getting zero Oscar nominations. You have to keep doing what you're doing. Just keep going no matter what.

7. Stay Connected With Your Family

If you are a mother and jogs between 8 to 10 working hours and attending to your family, you hold a soft spot in Meryl's heart. In a podcast, she recounts how her priority was only on those roles that were both location and time-friendly to have quality time with her family.

8. Make the Mold, Then Advance It

After developing an understanding of yourself, set your standards and navigate your way through, which you'll rely on. It is about what feels suitable to you, not what you've been told. Throughout her 45-year career, Meryl has created and reinvented herself, thus ensuring that she improves her talent, craft, and ideas and remaining relevant in Hollywood.

9. Good Things Take Time

In modern society, delayed progress is no progress, and the patient feels worthless than virtuous. Nonetheless, Meryl's career journey is an excellent example of how good things take time because it wasn't until 10 years after acting that she gained the recognition she deserved. Persist at it until you get to where you want to be.

10. Stay Humble

Meryl Streep often referred to as the best actress of her generation, would have within her rights succumbed to the luxuries of being a celebrity. But she chose to stay grounded, and as she told Vogue Magazine that she tried as much to live an ordinary life as when you do your own taming, you cannot get spoilt.

Conclusion

Having has built a successful career from the bottom through her appearances and roles in films and other avenues, Meryl Strip has become an iconic influence that seamlessly defines how you can hit the top by just being you.

Chapter 21:

10 Habits of Successful Traders

Becoming a successful trader is the dream of every business person. It is the crux of the art of doing business and only a handful of traders attain it. Trade has its ups and downs and a lot is required of you if you are to make it.

Here are ten habits of successful traders:

1. They Are Well Connected

Connections could be just what you are lacking for you to have that boom you have yearning. Doing business in urban areas is not a walk in the park. Successful traders seek partnerships with celebrities who help them market their products or services.

When you have a good relationship with influential people, they will channel customer traffic your way. Businesses with public figures as their brand ambassadors are more likely to do well in a highly competitive industry.

2. They Are Good Managers

Successful traders believe in themselves managing their trade. It is very difficult to find an unsupervised trustworthy employee who will steer a business to success. This has made successful traders learn to manage their business even if they were armatures at the beginning.

Over time, they manage to perfect their management skills and require external help less often. Management requires practice and successful traders do not give up learning it. Some even enroll in colleges to learn management skills that they will implement in their businesses.

3.   They Are Risk-Takers

The art of doing trade sometimes requires extreme decisions involving risks. The return on investment of risky ventures is high, although few traders are ready to wade into such territories. This makes only a handful of traders successful.

Taking calculated risks is the habit of successful traders. They have a backup mechanism to cushion their businesses in the event of an unanticipated loss. The underlying principle in investment is that the higher the risk the higher the returns.

4.   They are Knowledgeable About Their Market

Knowledge is power and successful traders use this tool in their businesses. You need accurate and precise information about the market if you want to meet its needs. Successful traders do not sit back to wait for information but instead hunt for it themselves.

With the right data, they implement the right strategies. Unlike merchants who are in business aimlessly, successful traders have relevant information about the market they operate in at their fingertips.

5.   They Take Customer Feedback Seriously

Feedback is an important aspect of communication. Serious traders end up successful because they incorporate this in their businesses. They always seek client responses on how they enjoyed their goods or services. Routine asking for feedback is not in vain. It is aimed at improving their services or products for consumer consumption. When clients observe that their feedback was taken seriously, they will be motivated to use their products once more. Feedback is very powerful in sealing the success of any trade.

6. They Conform To The Emerging Trends

The needs of the market are ever-evolving and those in business should learn to evolve with them. This is a common habit of successful traders. They will go the extra mile to provide a new service to meet market demand.

The success of traders in competitive sectors of the economy is pegged on their adapting to new styles. They will be the first to stock clothes in fashion or the latest mobile devices. It is such stock that will move fast and they will realize higher revenues.

7. They Are Patient

Sometimes business could be at a low season. This does not qualify the traders to quit the business. Like everything else, business too has its off-peak days. Great patience is needed to survive this season – a trait successful traders have no shortage of.

Patience is required to grow a business steadily through the stages of growth until it breaks even and starts earning profit. Thereafter, the same business will pass the ceiling and register huge profit margins.

8. They Rarely Give Credit

As much as traders may want to give credit to maintain customer loyalty, the success of a business may not be realized if they overdo it. There are several factors that successful business people consider before allowing credit and being reckless about it is not one of them.

Customer loyalty is not guaranteed because you allow credit. It may make you be bankrupt and close shop. Successful traders give discounts when their clients make purchases instead of giving credit recklessly.

9. They Maintain An Excellent Relationship With Their Suppliers

The relationship between traders and their suppliers is as equally important as that between them and their customers. Successful traders build bridges with their suppliers over time even up to the point of getting goods on credit to sell and pay later.

Such strong relationships with suppliers ensure these traders never run out of stock. Customers will always find goods from their stores and business will run smoothly. This makes a great difference in trade to crown them successful.

10. They Are Law-Abiding

Trade is legitimate in all jurisdictions worldwide except that the items of trade are illegal in that country. This informs the success of a business. It should conform to existing laws and be subject to inspection by authorities.

Successful traders are law-abiding. They pay taxes and seek a license to operate. This insulates their businesses from legal action against them. Their acceptance of regulation will help them remain open when their peers are evading crackdowns on illicit trade. They attract more customers because of their consistency in operation.

In conclusion, successful traders are tied to the hip by these ten habits. They have propelled them to their success. To be successful like they are, implement them and watch your star in trade rise.

Chapter 22:

__Be Motivated by Challenge__

You have an easy life and a continuous stream of income, you are lucky! You have everything you and your children need, you are lucky! You have your whole future planned ahead of you and nothing seems to go in the other direction yet, you are lucky!

But how far do you think this can go? What surety can you give yourself that all will go well from the start to the very end?

Life will always have a hurdle, a hardship, a challenge, right there when you feel most satisfied. What will you do then?

Will you give up and look for an escape? Will you seek guidance? Or will you just give up and go down a dark place because you never thought something like this could happen to you?

Life is full of endless possibilities and an endless parade of challenges that make life no walk in the park.

You are different from any other human being in at least one attribute. But your life isn't much different than most people's. You may be less fortunate or you may be the luckiest, but you must not back down when life strikes you.

This world is a cruel place and a harsh terrain. But that doesn't mean you should give up whenever you get hit in the back. That doesn't mean you don't catch what the world throws at you.

Do you know what you should do? Look around and observe for examples. Examples of people who have had the same experiences as you had and what good or bad things did they do? You will find people on both extremes.

You will find people who didn't have the courage or guts to stand up to the challenge and people who didn't have the time to give up but to keep pushing harder and harder, just to get better at what they failed the last time.

The challenges of life can never cross your limits because the limits of a human being are practically infinite. But what feels like a heavy load, is just a shadow of your inner fear dictating you to give up.

But you can't give up, right? Because you already have what you need to overcome this challenge too. You just haven't looked into your backpack of skills yet!

If you are struggling at college, go out there and prove everyone in their wrong. Try to get better grades by putting in more hours little by little.

If people take you as a non-social person, try to talk to at least one new person each day.

If you aren't getting good at a sport, get tutorials and try to replicate the professionals step by step and put in all your effort and time if you truly care for the challenge at hand.

The motivation you need is in the challenge itself. You just need to realize the true gains you want from each stone in your path and you will find treasures under every stone.

Chapter 23:

10 Reasons Money Can't Buy You Happiness

I'm sure you have heard this statement before, that "Money can't buy happiness.", but have you stopped to think about why it might be so? Many of us chase money and that high paying job because we believe that it will bring us wealth which will in turn make us happy. We do it because it is what society tells us we should be doing. That we should trade all our time and energy to make money no matter how many sacrifices we have to make with regards to our friendships, relationships, and so on.

It is true that a certain income level and money in the bank is required to allow us to have a comfortable standard of living, which could make life quite nice for us. But beyond that, it will be tough to derive happiness from just sheer truckloads of money alone, as we will soon find out.

1. Our Happiness Is Not Derived From Material Things

This is arguably the most important yet easily overlooked aspect when it comes to dealing with money. While most of us will have desires to live in a dream home, owning the ultimate luxury car, and buying the greatest gifts we can buy when we're rich, we fail to realize that the process of acquisition of material things is a futile effort. It is always thrilling to be on the forefront of owning the latest material good on the market, but the excitement you have for a product usually fades away pretty quickly once you have them in your hands. We acclimatize very quickly to what we have, and we search for the next thing almost immediately. This seemingly endless chase for happiness would seem like a carrot on a stick, always dangling it's juiciness in front of you but you never get to taste it. If you look around at the things you have in your house, you will know what I mean. All the stuff that was once intriguing to you now no longer has the same effect of joy and happiness that it once had. Bottom line is that there is no amount of stuff you can acquire that will ever make you truly happy.

2. Money Cannot Buy You Relationships

We fail to realize the power of relationships when it comes to the happiness equation. Happiness can easily be derived from thriving relationships. Relationships that serve to enrich our lives in all aspects of it. When we are in a relationship with someone who loves and cares for us unconditionally, there is no amount of money that can buy you that feeling. The same goes for friendships and family. Having people that support you in your endeavors, grieve with you when you experience loss, or just someone you can talk to, to share your feelings of excitement, sorrow, and all the different ranges of emotions, those are the moments that truly matter in life.

3. Money Could Lure Disingenuous People

While some may argue that you can buy friendships by paying people to be around you, I am pretty sure most of you wouldn't want to go down that path. You know that these people are not hanging around you because they like you, but because they like what you have in your pocket. Genuine relationships are ones that will last even when you don't have a dime left in your back account. When all else fails, you will want to have these people around you for support.

4. You Will Never Feel Like You have Enough Money

Chasing money as a substitute for happiness is a tricky thing. We all think we need $1 million dollars in our bank account to be happy, but as soon as we hit that milestone, something just doesn't feel quite right. We feel empty inside, we feel like maybe it's not enough, so we set a bigger target of $2 million. But that day will come too and again we will feel like something is amiss. The cycle repeats itself until we finally realize that deriving happiness from a monetary goal is also a futile effort.

5. Money Only Helps To Improve Your Standard of Living

Instead of using money as bait for happiness, use it for what it really is for - survival, food, clothing, a roof over your head, and the occasional splurge on something you like. Beyond that, look elsewhere for happiness. I am here to tell you that it is human nature for us to feel like we never have enough of something, and that includes money. We have been programmed to always want and need more. More of everything. We compare to people more successful than us and think we need to live like them in order to be happy. Don't make the same mistake as everyone else. Find a comfortable amount you need for survival and retirement, and the rest is bonus.

6. Making Money Requires Sacrifices

Unless you're a trust fund baby, or money falls from the sky, or you managed to strike a jackpot, constantly putting money above all else requires time and effort to earn. Working 12 hour shifts, 7 days a week is no easy feat. You will see your youth fly by and your other priorities fall by the wayside. By the time you've earned the desired income of your dreams, you may well find that a few decades have passed and you're standing on top of the mountain, alone, with no one to share that experience with. No one who may be able to travel with you or even spend that money with you. Unless you consciously try for a balanced work-life, you will find it quite a lonesome experience.

7. The Simple Pleasures In Life Doesn't Require That Much Money

Spending time with your family, going out for coffee with friends, having a chill board games night on the weekends with enthusiasts like yourself, you will find that all these activities brings us closer to the emotional world. The emotional and spiritual connection we have with fellow human beings that bring us laughter, joy, sadness, and happiness. We fail to realize that the happiest moments we can create doesn't require that much money. It just requires planning and some food. Stop chasing the dream vacation halfway around the world for happiness. It is underneath you all along.

8. You Lack the Happiness Mindset

Happiness is merely a feeling, and feelings can be created by choice. Money can't fix your emotional problems, it can only buy you therapy. Ultimately, it's your attitude and mindset that determines your level of happiness that you experience. If you always see the glass half empty, no amount of money can make you see the glass as half full.

9. You Don't Feel Grateful for The Things Money Buy You

We take for granted the things we have acquired so far and only look towards the next shiny object. Being grateful for our hard-earned money has bought us thus far should be our number one priority. Treasure the bed you bought that you can sleep comfortably in, be thankful for the television you have that allows you to stream your favourite shows on demand, be grateful for the roof that houses all these items and protects you from the elements.

10. We Fall into The If-Then Trap of Chasing Money

How many times do you have the thought that the next promotion you receive will be the happiest moment of your life. Or perhaps that your boss will give me a raise if you turn this project in successfully. If we only chase our paychecks rather than chase fulfillment, we are running the wrong race in life.

Remember these important points the next time you work for money. Yes, having money is important, but it should not adversely affect your ability to live a fulfilling life. There are a million other things that are just as equally important if you're chasing happiness.

Chapter 24:

What To Do When You Feel Like Your Work is not Good Enough

Feeling like your work is not good enough is very common; your nerves can get better of you at any time throughout your professional life. There is nothing wrong with nerves; It tells you that you care about improving and doing well. Unfortunately, too much nervousness can lead to major self-doubt, and that can be crippling. You are probably very good at your work, and when even once you take a dip, you think that things are not like how they seem to you. If this is something you're feeling, then you're not alone, and this thing is known as Imposter Syndrome. This term is used to describe self-doubt and inadequacy. This one thing leaves people fearing that there might be someone who will expose them. The more pressure you apply to yourself, the more dislocation is likely to occur. You create more anxiety, which creates more fear, which creates more self-doubt. You don't have to continue like this. You can counter it.

Beyond Work

If your imposter syndrome affects you at work, you should take some time out and start focusing on other areas of your life. There are chances that there is something in your personal life that is hindering your work life. This could be anything your sleep routine, friends, diet, or even your relationships. There is a host of external factors that can affect your performance. If there are some boxes you aren't ticking, then there is a high chance of you not performing well at work.

You're Better Than You Think

When you're being crippled by self-doubt, the first thing you have to think about is why you were hired in the first place. The interviewers saw something in you that they believed would improve the business.

So, do you think they would recruit someone who can't do the job? No, they saw your talent, they saw something in you, and you will come good.

When you find yourself in this position, take a moment to write down a few things that you believe led to you being in the role you are now. What did those recruiters see? What did your boss recognize in you? You can also look back on a period of time where you were clicking and felt victorious. What was different then versus now? Was there an external issue like diet, exercise, socializing, etc.?

Check Yourself Before You Wreck Yourself

A checklist might be of some use to you. If you have a list to measure yourself against, then it gives you more than just one thing to judge yourself against. We're far too quick to doubt ourselves and criticize harshly.

The most obvious checklist in terms of work is technical or hard skills, but soft skills matter, too. It's also important to remember that while you're technically proficient now, things move quickly, and you'll reach a point where everything changes, and you have to keep up. You might not ever excel at something, but you can accept the change and adapt to the best of your ability.

It matters that you're hard-working, loyal, honest, and trustworthy. There's more to judge yourself on than just your job. Even if you make a mistake, it's temporary, and you can fix it.

Do you take criticism well? Are you teachable? Easy to coach? Soft skills count for something, which you can look to even at your lowest point and recognize you have strengths.

When you're struggling through a day, week, or even a month, take one large step backward and think about what it is you're unhappy with. What's causing your unhappiness, and how can you improve it?

It comes down to how well you know yourself. If you're clear on what your values are and what you want out of life, then you're going to be fine. If the organization you work for can't respect your values and harness your strengths, then you're better off elsewhere. So, it is extremely important to take time out for that self check-in there could be times you talk to yourself in negative light. Checking in with yourself regularly and not feeding yourself negativity could be one-step forward.

Chapter 25:

Six Habits of The Mega-Rich

There are rich people then there are the mega-rich. The distinction between them is as clear as day. The former are still accumulating their wealth while the latter is beyond that. Their focus is no longer on themselves but humanity. Their view of things is through the prism of business and not employment. Their business enterprises are well established and their level of competition is unmatched. They are at the top of the pyramid and have a clear view of things below.

Here are six habits of the mega-rich:

1. They Have a Diversified Investment Portfolio

The mega-rich are ardent followers of the saying "do not put all your eggs in one basket." They have stakes in every type of business across many world economies beginning with their country. Their patriotism makes them not leave out their countries when they do business.

With diversified risk across various sectors of the economy, they can remain afloat even during tough economic times. Their companies and businesses also yield high returns because of proper management and their diversification.

2. They Are Generous

The mega-rich people are generous to a fault. They run foundations and non-governmental organizations in their name with a cause to help humanity. It indicates their generosity and desire to help the most vulnerable and needy in society. Generosity is a hard trait to trace these days and it distinguishes the mega-rich from kind people.

The generosity of mega-rich people seeks to help the needy permanently by showing them how to fish instead of giving them fish. Such an act liberates families from poverty and promises a brighter future to the younger generation.

3. They Are Neither Petty Nor Trivial

Pettiness is not the character of mega-rich people. They do not have time for small squabbles and fights. Instead, they use their energy in pursuit of more productive goals. Their minds always think of their next big move and ways to improve their businesses. They do not have time to engage in non-issues.

Mega-rich investors do not undertake trivial investments. Their businesses are major leaving people marveling at its grandiose. Jeff Benzos took a trip to space and the world was amazed. The impact the ilk of Benzos has in the world economy is unmatched; securities exchanges and global trade shakes whenever such people make a business move.

4. They Have A Clean Public Image

The mega-rich people manage to maintain a scandalous-free public image. This is crucial for their success. When was the last time you came across a character-damaging story of a wealthy person? It is difficult to recall. Perception tends to stick in the minds of people more than reality. This makes it important for them to guard their reputation with their life. If you are on the path of joining the exclusive club of the mega-rich, begin cleaning up your reputation if it is a mess. Build a new public image that will portray you as a better person to the world. Mega-rich people intimidate by their angel-like reputations and immense influence on their social status.

5. They Have Great Character

A man's character precedes his reputation. Every wealthy person upgrades his/hers. The mega-rich treasure character too much because they are unable to buy it at any price. It is invaluable. Characterlessness is a type of poverty only curable the hard way. There is no shortcut to it except tireless and intentional channeling of your efforts to strengthen it. A great character is an asset envied by the great and mighty because most of them fall short of it. There are untold stories of the efforts mega-rich people put to build their character. This has formed part of their routine and life habit.

6. They Champion Global Causes

Mega-rich people are champions of social justice and world causes like climate change and global warming. They give their contribution towards global causes without any self-interest. They are at the forefront offering support in whatever capacity.

They invest in these worthy causes because of the duty of corporate social responsibility they owe the world. It is not a debt they pay but an act they do gladly because they have the best interest of the world at heart.

These six habits of the mega-rich have formed their lifestyle. Walk in their footsteps if you want to become like them. You will command respect from everybody. Your business moves shall determine world market trends and you shall set the pace in every sector of the economy.

Chapter 26:

10 Habits of Nancy Pelosi

You can't acknowledge prominent women in the history of American politics without mentioning Nancy Pelosi. Nancy Pelosi is a well-known American politician and a Democrat. She is the current Speaker of the House of representatives for yet another term under President Biden's administration-which marks nearly 50-years in politics.

Pelosi began her political journey in 1976 when she was elected to the Democratic Party National Committee. In 1977, she rose to become the party's leader in California. Pelosi has held the positions of Minority Whip and Minority Leader. Curious of how she rose to such prominence?

Here are 10 Habits of Nancy Pelosi.

1. Establish and Pursue Your Dreams

According to Pelosi, you can't succeed in life without a clear vision and willingness to pursue it. Looking at her political career journey, it's evidence that she has achieved what she desired as a successful politician. Pelosi noted in an interview that you would fail to realize your goals if your focus is on things that don't align with your desires.

2. It Doesn't Matter What Gender You Are

Pelosi believes that it makes no difference whether you are a man or a woman; as long as you have the necessary skills, you can flourish in any role. She urges women to be courageous enough to challenge the notion of "male dominated roles." Pelosi joined politics when patriarchy was at its core and later became the first female Speaker of the House of Representatives.

3. Work Collaboratively With Others

Pelosi acknowledges the essence of working with other people who has the same affiliation as you-in this case, her democrat party members. To achieve great things, you will need the help and input of others, particularly those with more skills and experience. However, it would be best if you only worked with those who believe in you.

4. Be Your Own Best Sensationalist

Self-promotion is something frowned about, but someone has to do it. Do you know who doesn't hold back when it comes to bragging about how terrific she is? Pelosi herself. At a press conference in 2017, Pelosi flaunted how she was a master legislator, strategic, politically adept leader, among others. If you don't publicize yourself out there, who will?

5. Enjoy the Fight

There are two-way contented warriors in DC, and then there is Nancy Pelosi. In an interview, when asked to respond to Dianne Feinstein's statement that women in politics should be prepared to take a punch, she responded with a broad smile, "you must also know how to throw it too."

6. Keep Your Frenemies Closer

According to Pelosi, keep your frenemies closer enough to cooperate with when necessary. However, there is a dark, cold place for democrats like Rep. Moulton for his efforts to oust Pelosi earlier in 2018. "What do you call someone who seems 99% loyal? Disloyal!" In short, if you're going after Pelosi, you better win.

7. Be True to Your Authentic Self

When should you change your mind, and when should you stick to your guns? The answer to that all-time leadership question is not only "it depends," but also when it's right in the eyes of the public. Nancy demonstrates as she puts it, "sticking to your guns and not succumbing to needless pressure."

8. Money Talks

Money is power in politics and business; you must master the money game, as Pelosi has. Her political career has been defined by fundraising, both for her party and for individual candidates too. This is how you win hearts and list up your political allies.

9. Claim Your Place at the Table

Having spent years paddling up the ladder, expect no rush in endorsing Pelosi's replacement. As Molly Ball's book, "Pelosi" indicates, calling herself a "transitional leader" merely meant that those who wished to limit her term were naive. Did it just prove true? She exemplifies what it looks like when a woman doesn't care what other people think or call her—as long as you call her "madam speaker" one more time.

10. Leadership Is About Personal Experience

Consider this: politicians and toddlers have a lot in common, don't they? For Pelosi, having a large family and a leader necessitates being efficient with your time and getting things done. And also being patient enough when dealing with people who can throw tantrums and need to be taken care of.

Conclusion

Strong, powerful women like Nancy Pelosi demonstrates the importance of women's involvement in political processes. As a woman, embrace your power and value your experience enough to conquer a political battle that men take privilege in.

Chapter 27:

6 Tricks To Become More Aware Of Your Strengths

"Strength and growth come only through continuous effort and struggle." - Napoleon Hill.

While it is true that we tend to focus more on our weaknesses than on our strengths, it is also true that we should polish our strengths more than our weaknesses. This in no way means that we should consider ourselves superior to others and start looking away from that we have flaws. Unfortunately, most of us don't spend much time on self-reflection and self-awareness. But they are the vital aspects if we are thinking of improving ourselves in any way.

Here are 6 Tricks to become more aware of your strengths:

1. Decide to be more self-aware

Human beings are complicated creatures. Our minds are designed so that we tend to absorb more negative than positive thoughts about ourselves and others. For this reason, self-awareness is perhaps the most crucial thing in an individual's life. Self-awareness is the ability to look deep inside of yourself and monitor your emotions and reactions. It is the ability to allow yourself to be aware of your strengths, weaknesses, as well as your triggers, motivators, and other characteristics. We'll help you find a set of tricks and techniques that you can apply to polish your strengths in a self-awareness way; and how to use your strengths in a promising way.

2. Meditation:

The first thought that will come to your mind would be, "Is this person crazy? How can meditation help us improve our strengths?" But hear me out. The fresh breeze of the morning when everything is at peace, and you sit there inhaling all the good energy in and the bad energy out, your mind and thoughts would automatically become slow-paced and calm. Once you get to relax with yourself, you can analyze the things that have been happening in your life and develop possible solutions on how you can deal with them using your strengths. The positive energy and calming mood you will get after meditating would help you make your decisions wisely when you are under pressure and your mind is in chaos.

3. Labelling your thoughts:

More often, our thoughts reflect on our behavior and what makes us fail or succeed in life. People can genuinely relate to a situation where they could have possibly thought about a worst-case scenario, but in the end, nothing as such happened. Our anxiety and hopelessness don't come from the situation we are struggling with, but rather our thoughts make us believe in the worst possible things that could happen to us. But we're stronger than we give ourselves credit for. We have the power to control our negative thoughts and turn them into positive ones. We can list all the ideas and thinking that provide us with stress and tension and then label them as either useful or useless. If the particular thought is causing a significant effect in your life, you can work towards it to make your life better and less anxious. Know your priorities and take help from your strengths to tackle the problems.

4. **Befriending your fears:**

There's not a single person on this planet who isn't afraid of something. Be it the fear of losing your loved ones or any phobias of either animal, insects, heights, closed spaces, etc. There are also so many fears related to our self-worth and whether we are good enough, skilled enough, or deserving enough of anything. To accept these fears and work towards overcoming them is perhaps the most powerful thing one could do. It takes so much of a person's strength and willpower to befriend fear, reduce it, and finally eliminate it. Most of the time, we end up in situations that we always feared, and then we have to take quick actions and make wise decisions. To remain calm in such cases and use your strengths and experiences to tackle whatever's in front of you is a remarkable quality found in only a few. But we can also achieve and polish this quality by strengthening our minds and preparing ourselves to get us out of situations wisely and effectively. To be patient and look into the problems from every angle is the critical component of this one.

5. **Watching your own movie:**

Narrating your life experiences to yourself or a close friend and telling yourself and them how far you have come can boost your self-confidence immensely. You should go in flashbacks and try to remember all the details of your life. You will find that there were some moments you felt immense joy and some moments where you felt like giving up. But with all the strength that you were collecting along the way, you endured the possible tortures and struggles and challenges and eventually rose again. So you should focus and be well aware of how you tackle those situations, what powers you have, and the strengths that couldn't let you give up but face everything. Once you have found the answers to the above questions, like for example, it was your patience and bravery that helped you through it, or it was your wise and speedy decisions that made it all effective, you can understand what strengths you have and make use of them later in life too.

6. Motivate yourself:

We should stop looking for others to notice how great we did or stop waiting for a round of applause or a pat on the back from them. Instead, we should motivate ourselves every time we fall apart, and we should have the energy to pick ourselves back up again. The feeling of satisfaction we get after completing a task or helping someone, that feeling is what we should strive for. We should become proud of ourselves and our strengths, as well as our weaknesses, that they helped us transform into the person we are today. We should never feel either superior or inferior to others. Everyone has their own pace and their own struggles. Our strengths should not only be for ourselves but for others too. Kindness, empathy, hospitality, being there for people, patience, courage, respect are all the qualities that one must turn into their strengths.

Conclusion:

The key to perfection is self-awareness. There's a fine line between who you are and who you strive to become; it can be achieved by becoming aware of your strengths, polishing them, and creating a sense of professional as well as personal development. Your strengths motivate you to try new things, achieve new skills, become a better version of yourself. Your strengths are what keeps you positive, motivated, help you to maintain your stress better, aid you in your intuitive decision making, and command you to help others as well. It inspires you to become a better person.

Chapter 28:

Seven Habits of Mentally Strong People

Mentally strong people also have great character and charming personalities because they can handle what ordinary people may not handle. Mental strength is the most desired trait by most people. To some, it is innate but others cultivate it over time through education or the school of life. Whichever way it is acquired, there are underlying habits that mentally strong people share.

Here are seven habits of mentally strong people:

1. They Are Forgiving

To err is human but forgiveness is divine. Forgiveness is difficult for most people to commit. It is seen as a sign of weakness but this is a fallacy. The contrary is true. Forgiveness is a measure of strength. When one person grossly transgresses another, the offended party will seek vengeance. He/she feels justified to revenge and until the offender 'pays' for his mistakes, the spirit of the offended will know no rest.

Mentally strong people are capable of forgiveness. This distinguishes them from the rest of the population. They understand that there is no point in re-visiting a matter when they can shelf it and prevent its repeat in the future. It does not mean that the offender has the license to continue hurting the other person. Instead, forgiveness sets the precedence that you are unaffected by the acts of an inconsiderate person. It demonstrates that your reasoning and emotions are not manipulated at will by someone who hurts you.

The next time someone wrongs you, let vengeance take the back seat and reason prevail over your actions. It is what mentally strong people do.

2. They Are Readers

There is nothing new under the sun. Everything that happens is a repetition of something that once occurred. To acquaint yourself with how history judged those who were once in your shoes, flip the pages of books and learn the signs of the time.

The habit of reading is not only for the literate. Even the illiterate can read, not books but the signs of the time and the harsh judgment of history on failures of men. Mentally strong people are wise not to learn from their mistakes but those of others. They unlearn the habits of failures and learn those of the successful.

Readership is a dynamic habit that is perfected by the mentally strong. They read the prevailing situations and adjust their actions accordingly. Reading builds the wealth of experience in life and prepares one on what action to take when confronted by a situation.

3. They Accept Criticism and Correction

Acceptance of correction from an authority displays humility. Correction and positive criticism are not to display your ignorance to the public but instead to inform you on a matter you were once ignorant about. Many people take criticism negatively and want to justify their actions. It is not always about being right or wrong – a concept that most people miss.

Embracing correction distinguishes mentally strong people from the faint-hearted who always rush to justify their acts.

The intelligence of the mentally strong is belittled when they engage in supremacy battles. They rise above the hate and become big brothers/sisters. Only a handful of a population can own up to their misinformation on a matter and humbly accept correction. Mentally strong people can display such levels of maturity.

4. They Are Not Easily Discouraged

It takes a lot to discourage mentally strong people. While ordinary people are stoppable in their tracks, it is not the same for the mentally strong. They are resilient to the adversity of whatever nature. They pursue their targets viciously and settle at nothing short of victory.

Mentally strong people may face a thousand ways to die but survive every one of them. They have the proverbial nine lives of the cat. Their determination is unmatched making them the envy of their peers who give up easily when challenged.

The majority of people in their curriculum vitae say that they can work under pressure. Unfortunately, their breaking point reaches sooner than expected. In the face of immense pressure at work, they yield to frivolous and unrealistic demands meted on them by busybodies. This is not the portion of the mentally strong.

5. They Are Innovative

Mentally strong people are not satisfied with the status quo. They always seek to unsettle the ordinary way of doing things. The traditional handling of affairs does not ogre well with them. There is always a new way of doing things.

Their mental strength is partly responsible for the adventurous spirit. The mentally endowed put their brains to work in solving human problems. They innovate simple life hacks, technology and come up with homemade solutions that were unknown before.

Innovation is not limited to the complicated science of experts. It also involves finding the simplest ways of solving problems in society. Innovation is habitual for mentally strong people.

6.   They See The Bigger Picture

Life is a hunt for resources. Similar to the Lion, Mentally strong people do not lose focus of the antelope because of a dashing squirrel. To them, the point of reference is always the bigger picture. They interrogate every matter diligently to read between the lines because the devil always lies in the details.

It is not a matter of the emotions invoked in a discussion but the quality of reasoning devoid of any feelings. Mentally strong people can sieve needs from wants and decant fallacies from discussions.

7.   They Are Bold

Fortune favors the bold. It is one thing to be decisive and another to boldly speak out your thoughts. Timidity is for mental infants (no offense). Mentally strong people are not afraid of giving their inputs in forums whenever required to because they speak from a point of knowledge.

Fearlessly talking about social ills and injustices is uncommon even among the political class. They lack the mental strength to engage fruitfully in matters of national importance. The bold is unafraid of how they may be challenged by other people because they are capable of seeing everybody's point of view. They appreciate the diversity in opinions.

The above are seven habits of mentally strong people. Mental strength wields untold power to those who possess it.

Chapter 29:

How to Deal with Stress Head On? 7 Things You Can Start Today

Drop your shoulders, release your tongue from your palate. Unclench your teeth and let your brows relax. You see, this is how stressed you are all the time, you forget completely about how it is affecting your body.

In this roaring river of the 21st century, we are all feeling the tide rising and falling 24/7. It will be a white lie if any of you claim to never feel stressed. We are all under varying degrees of stress all the time.

So what is stress exactly? Stress is not merely a stimulus or a physical response of our bodies but a process by which we appraise and cope with environmental threats and challenges. When expressed in short bursts or taken as a challenge, stressors may have positive effects. However, if stress is threatening or prolonged, it can be harmful for us.

So how then do we handle it?

It seems like quite a drag for most of us and pretty annoying a lot of the time, but here are several ways we can deal with it and come out of it stronger than before.

7 Tips to Deal with stress and anxiety

Number 1: Go To Bed Early and Wake up Early

Have you heard the quote "Early to Bed, early to rise, makes a man healthy, wealthy and wise."? When was the last time you went to sleep early? I believe that going to bed early is something we all know we need to do but hardly ever do.

Starting your day off early has many wonderful biological effects. Mornings tend to be cool, silent, serene, and distraction-free. This calmness helps bring our stress levels down and prepares us for the day ahead. By practicing some deep breathing techniques in the morning, it will also aid in flow and circulation throughout our bodies, something that is good for the mind and soul.

Number 2: Start Practicing Yoga or meditation

Yoga and meditation, while they are two separate practices, they overlap in many key areas. Yoga poses are great for us to engage with our bodies, to stretch out our muscles, tight sections of our bodies, and to help us focus on our breath at all times. Each yoga pose targets a unique meridian of our bodies, many allowing us to release tensions that might otherwise have built up without realizing. You can try simple poses such as a child pose or shavasana, or downward dog, to get yourself started.

Meditation on the other hand focuses stilling the mind through focus on the breath as well. Letting our thoughts flow freely, we are able to acknowledge the stressors we face without judgement. Try out some guided mindfulness meditation practices to get your started.

Number 3: Having Proper Time Management

Many of us overlook the importance of proper time management. We often let our crazy schedules overwhelm us. By being unorganized with our time, we are also unorganized with our emotions. If we let our calendar be filled with chaos, there is no doubt that we will feel like chaos as well. Stress levels will be bound to rise. Have proper blocks of time dedicated to each task in your day. Trust me you will feel a whole lot more in control of everything.

Number 4: Make time for your hobbies

We should all strive to live a happy and balanced life. If work is the only thing on our agenda, we will have no outlet to destress, relax, recharge, and be ready to face new challenges that might tax our physical and mental abilities.

Whatever your hobbies are: baking, tennis, crafting, surfboarding, or even shopping, as long as you plan them in your schedule and do them, you will definitely feel a whole lot better about everything. Let out all the steam, stress, anxieties, as you engage in your hobbies, or even just forget about them for a minute. Give yourself the space to breathe and just enjoy doing the fun things in life. Life isn't just all about work. Play is equally important too.

Number 5: Music is food for your soul

Music has many therapeutic qualities. If you feel your stress levels rising, consider popping your earbuds into your ears and playing your favorite songs on spotify. If you are looking for calm, you may want to consider listening to some chill music as well.

The kind of your music you listen to will have a direct effect on your mood and the way you feel. So choose your playlists wisely. Don't go heavy metal or goth, unless of course it helps calm you down.

Number 6: Start Cleaning your clutter

This may seem like I am quoting a movie where the stressed teenage girl decides to clean her room when she is feeling low. I'd say movies are made out of someone's real experience.

Cleaning your room or clutter can be one of the best therapies.

A messy space is a recipe for anxiety and stress. When we see clutter, we feel cluttered. Once you clear all the stuff you don't need, you will feel much lighter instantly.

Number 7: Allow nature to heal you

Nature is amusing and wonderful. Everything in nature is closer to our basic making than anything that we are dealing with today. So try getting close to nature, it will make you feel relaxed and at the same time enable you to enrich your brain.

Watch the sun setting into the sky and wake up to look at the colors at dawn.
There is nothing more beautiful in this world that we get to experience every single day no matter where we are on this earth.

Take a stroll in your favourite park, go for a cycle, a jog, or even just a stroll with your pet. Allow nature to melt away your stress and bring your peace.

Final Thoughts

Stressors are a part of life. Something we cannot escape from. But if we put in place some healthy habits and practices, we can reduce and release those negativities from our bodies, cleansing us to take on more stress in the future.

Chapter 30:

Happy People Don't Hold on To Grudges

Holding a grudge is when you harbor anger, bitterness, resentment, or other negative feelings long after someone has done something to hurt you. Usually, it's in response to something that's already occurred. Other times a grudge may develop after simply perceiving that someone is against you or means you harm—whether or not they do. Grudges also often feature persistent rumination about the person and/or incident at the center of your ill-will.

While we don't often like to admit it, holding a grudge is a common way some people respond to the feeling that they've been wronged. If you're still mad well after a precipitating incident, you may be holding on to those negative feelings for too long, sometimes well after other people typically would have let them go. You may remember multiple past bad acts and relive those experiences every time you think about or interact with that person—either making your displeasure abundantly clear to them or keeping your true feelings to yourself. You might be intentionally holding a grudge, but sometimes you aren't even aware of it.

But whatever your intentions or the cause of your bitterness, holding a grudge can end up hurting you as much as the person who inspired it. Learn more about how clinging to anger can impact you emotionally, physically, and socially, as well as how to begin to let go of your grudges and cope with anger more healthily. From early childhood on, holding a grudge is one-way people respond to negative feelings and events. This reaction is particularly common when you think someone has done something intentionally, callously, or thoughtlessly to hurt you, especially if they don't seem to care or make an attempt to apologize or make the situation right.

If you have low self-esteem, poor coping skills, were embarrassed by the hurt, and/or have a short temper, you may be even more likely to hold a grudge. While we all may fall into holding an occasional grudge, some people may be more prone to hanging on to resentments or anger than other people. Sometimes, holding grudges—and blaming others—may be a form of self-protection. In the same vein, some people may be more conscious that they are stoking feelings of bitterness than others, which may be unaware of their role in keeping their anger alive. Lasting bitterness can grow from a variety of issues—large and small—as well.

Chapter 31:

Why You've Come Too Far To Quit

Remember the first day of school, when someone bullied you for being too nerdy, or for being too whiny. What did you feel when some called you a Four-eye for wearing glasses? What did you do then? How did you answer them? You didn't! Right? Why?

Because you weren't strong enough then to tackle anyone. Because you didn't have any experience to tell you what to do next.

But your parents told you to stop crying and keep doing your thing and one day, everything will be secondary. So you kept your line, didn't indulge in anything anyone else said and you got through that time.

This is the definition of life. Life is a sequence of events that bully you at every corner. But you cannot give up on life, because someone put a dent on your new car or if someone spilled coffee on your shirt.

Things happen because life happens, and you live your life for the things you want to achieve one day.

You dream because you hope for a better future, and that future is worth living for if you have suffered and felt the pain.

Nothing in this life is easy, but nothing is impossible. It may not be possible for you but at the same moment it might be happening for someone else in the world

You have come this far, to achieve the goals your set. You can't give up now only because you haven't seen it yet.

You breathe every day because you have to. Your success has the same needs! You need to give life everything that you got. Not on some days, but every day because it is not something you do when you feel like it, but you have to because you have to live on your terms. No one can dictate your life but only you.

When you feel like quitting, remember why you started it all. You started it to prove everyone wrong. You started it to shun your haters. You started to bully the bullies.

When you feel like quitting, remember, you have too much to fight for and very little to quit for.

When you get up in the morning, remember what you dreamt of last night. Remember your failures and give yourself a chance to prove yourself wrong.

Quitting is for those who are still the kid they were back then. Quitting is for those who still have the feeling that everything will get better on its own - It never does, and it never will. Only if you quit the quitting attitude and start taking initiative for your ultimate dream.

The best you can be is by the best effort you put into being the protagonist of your story. Become the writer of your story. If you want your story to remain average, remain the same person you were a day before.

If your heart tells you to quit, rev up your heart to do one pick one more step towards your penultimate goal. Dictate your heart how bad do you want it.

If you are still the kid who still thinks that things will happen no matter what I do, believe me, you are wrong. This whole attitude of not trying hard enough to achieve your goals is the biggest thing wrong with an average human. But you are not an average human.

The average human wouldn't have the guts to pursue the dream in the first place. An average human wouldn't dream big in the first place. An average human would have given up on the first setback of life and went down a deep hole, only to avoid the problems. But it never is the solution to anything.

Build the guts to keep going no matter what happens. Life will beat you up at every interval. You might have a big setback after every brief moment of happiness.

You might lose friends, family, and everyone you ever cared for. People who were once standing shoulder to shoulder with you might not even care to say your name if they think you don't need what you are striving for. But they don't have a say in your future. It's you who has everything to care for. Everything to account for. So don't give up only because everyone else gave up on you. You are still alive and trying.

Give yourself every chance, to win. Give your life every chance for it to matter. Avail every stone to keep the bullies away, but not by mirroring the act, but your efforts for your goal and they will bow down one day.

Chapter 32:

How To Set Smart Goals

Setting your goals can be a tough choice. It's all about putting your priorities in such a way that you know what comes first for you. It's imperative to be goal-oriented to set positive goals for your present and future. You should be aware of your criteria for setting your goals. Make sure your plan is attainable in a proper time frame to get a good set of goals to be achieved in your time. You would need hard work and a good mindset for setting goals. Few components can help a person reach their destination. Control what you choose because it will eternally impact your life.

To set a goal to your priority, you need to know what exactly you want. In other words, be specific. Be specific in what matters to you and your goal. Make sure that you know your fair share of details about your idea, and then start working on it once you have set your mind to it. Get a clear vision of what your goal is. Get a clear idea of your objective. It is essential to give a specification to your plan to set it according to your needs.

Make sure you measure your goals. As in, calculate the profit or loss. Measure the risks you are taking and the benefits you can gain from them. In simple words, you need to quantify your goals to know what order to set them into. It makes you visualize the amount of time it will take or the energy to reach the finish line. That way, you can calculate your goals and their details. You need to set your mind on the positive technical growth of your goal. That is an essential step to take to put yourself to the next goal as soon as possible.

If you get your hopes high from the start, it may be possible that you will meet with disappointment along the way. So, it would be best if you made sure that your goals are realistic and achievable. Make sure your goal is within reach. That is the reality check you need to force in your mind that is your goal even attainable? Just make sure it is, and everything will go as planned. It doesn't mean to set small goals. There is a difference between big goals and unrealistic goals. Make sure to limit your romantic goals, or else you will never be satisfied with your achievement.

Be very serious when setting your goals, especially if they are long-term goals. They can impact your life in one way or another. It depends on you how you take it. Make sure your goals are relevant. So, that you can gain real benefit from your goals. Have your fair share of profits from your hard work and make it count. Always remember why the goal matters to you. Once you get the fundamental idea of why you need this goal to be achieved, you can look onto a bigger picture in the frame. If it doesn't feel relevant, then there is no reason for you to continue working for. Leave it as it is if it doesn't give you what you applied for because it will only drain your energy and won't give you a satisfactory outcome.

Time is an essential thing to keep in focus when working toward your goals. You don't want to keep working on one thing for too long or too short. So, keep a deadline. Keep a limit on when to work on your goal. If it's worth it, give it your good timer, but if not, then don't even waste a second on it. They are just some factors to set your goals for a better future. These visionary goals will help you get through most of the achievements you want to get done with.

Chapter 33:

9 Habits of Successful Students

Successful students are made up of a common DNA. This is because they share a backbone – their success. In the words of Aristotle, *we are what we repeatedly do. Excellence, then, is not an act, but a habit.* Success is a habit that this clique of students has perfected meticulously.

Here are 9 habits of successful students:

1. <u>They Identify With Their Status</u>

It begins at the beginning. It is a paradox in itself. The start of the success of successful students (pun intended) is their acceptance that they are students of whatever discipline they are pursuing. When they correctly identify with their discipline, the journey begins.

Next, they identify with the institution/person under whose tutelage they are placed. Appreciating the expertise of their seniors is as important as it is that they are successful. No one crowns himself King; Kingmakers do crown him or her. In this case, the institution provides the opportunity for the student and teacher to meet.

Successful students, at all levels, identify with their centers of learning. Be it primary school, high school, technical-vocational colleges, or universities, successful students are proud of them (at least during the duration of their study).

2. They Have A Good Attitude

How does the attitude of students connect with their success? Again, why are successful students proud of where they learn? If they have a bad attitude towards their centers of learning, they will dislike their teachers – those responsible for imparting knowledge to them. As a result, whatever they learn will not stick.

Successful students are as good as their attitude is towards their teachers, institutions, and discipline of study. If you want to master your studies then change your attitude. A good attitude opens you up to greater possibilities. The possibilities that will be open to you are infinite.

3. They Relate Well With Their Tutors

The relationship between learners and their teachers should strictly be professional (there is the risk of unethical behavior if it crosses that line). When learners are in harmony with their tutors, learning is easier.

A good relationship between students and teachers breeds trust. Trust is the foundation upon which success is founded. The goodwill of both the teacher and the student is based on the relationship between them. The former being devoted to the latter's needs and the latter submissive to the former's instructions.

Ask top candidates of national examinations how their relationship with their teachers was and you will hear of nothing short of "the best."

4. They Are Willing To Go The Extra Mile

The story of successful students is akin to a fairytale in a fairyland. The prince does everything to protect his bride. He will go the extra mile to make her happy, to know her better, and even to cheer her up. With this infinite love, either of them is ready to move mountains for the sake of the other.

Successful students and their studies are like the groom and bride in the fairyland. The students do not mind going an extra mile for their bride (studies). They study late into the night, sacrifice their free time to grasp new concepts, and are even ready to forego short-time pleasures for the sake of their education.

This sacrifice is what distinguishes them from the rest of their peers.

5. They Are Inquisitive

Successful students are always curious about what they do not know. The unknown stirs curiosity in them; they are never content with the status quo. Their inquisitive nature is gold – a rare characteristic in most students. A majority of them are satisfied with what they know.

Their inquisitiveness births innovation. While settling for nothing short of the best, they try out new practices, re-design existing models and create new inventions. They stand out from their peers. Being inquisitive is not disrespect for authority or existing knowledge. On the contrary, it is appreciating the current principles and building on them to come up with something better.

6. They Have Focus

Their primary goal is clear and everything else is secondary. Successful students have a razor-sharp focus of the eagle, not distracted by anything that crosses their line.

A perfect real-life example is that of a hunting lion. When it settles on its prey from a herd, it chases it to the end. It can even pass other animals while chasing the specific target. The lion does not care whether the animal that crosses its path is better than its target. The only thing that matters is getting to its target.

When students decide to prioritize their education above any other interest, their energy and concentration are drawn to it. Success will be their cup of tea.

7.   They Do Their Due Dilligence

The art of assuming is foreign to successful students. They treat everything in their discipline with utmost care. They research on results of experiments and answer the whys that arise.

It is never said by their tutors that they neglected their duty of research. Successful students know their role and they play it well. They know where and when to stop. This makes them disciplined compared to their colleagues.

Their discipline is outstanding. Shape your discipline and you will join the exclusive club of successful students.

8.   Abide By The Book

Successful students stick to the rules of the game. This is important since it is not all students who manage to complete the race. Like any other commitment, learning requires agility. It has its own rules, the common and the silent rules. Most important are the unspoken rules that students are expected to abide by.

What is left unsaid, for example, is that students are not expected to be in romantic relationships because it will get in the way of their education.

9. <u>They Are Punctual</u>

Successful students keep time. Punctuality is the backbone of planning which is very important for focused people. Keeping time helps students avoid missing classes and group discussions or arriving very late for the same.

Success itself arrives punctually in the sense that it gives proportionate results to the input invested by those who court it. Successful students are the best timekeepers. Those who do not observe time have learned the hard way how to.

These 9 habits are what successful students do to make it to the top and stay there.

CPSIA information can be obtained
at www.ICGtesting.com
Printed in the USA
BVHW091353020222
627784BV00015B/1405